Salt & Pepper Shakers IV

IDENTIFICATION & VALUES

Helene Guarnaccia

COLLECTOR BOOKS

A Division of Schroeder Publishing, Co., Inc.

Dedication

To my husband, Paul, who is still carting more boxes than he cares to think of, and has driven thousands of miles for the never-ending hunt; who has stopped at so many flea markets and antique shops, that a normal four-hour drive turns into eight; I couldn't do it without him. He's still the "Salt of the Earth!"

The current values in this book should be used only as a guide. They are not intended to set prices, which vary from one section of the country to another. Auction prices as well as dealer prices vary greatly and are affected by condition as well as demand. Neither the author nor the publisher assumes responsibility for any losses that might be incurred as a result of consulting this guide.

Searching For A Publisher?

We are always looking for knowledgeable people considered to be experts within their fields. If you feel that there is a real need for a book on your collectible subject and have a large comprehensive collection, contact Collector Books.

COLLECTOR BOOKS
P.O. Box 3009
Paducah, Kentucky 42002-3009
www.collectorbooks.com

Copyright © 1993 by Helene Guarnaccia

Table of Contents

Susie Frank. Pasadena, California. A fantastic earthquake-proof storage system.

Dot Gammon's Shaker Barn in Tennessee.

Nell Weathers' home in Memphis, Tennessee.

Home of Nigel Dalley, England.

Home of Jan and David Peters in Venice, California.

Clara and Hubert McHugh's dining room in Stroudsburg, Pennsylvania.

Salt & Pepper Shakers
...And How They Party

Richard Robar and Joyce Higbee of Salt Lake City, Utah, as Peek-a-Boos shakers by Van Tellingen. Shakers pictured above right.

Gloria Winslow of Long Island, New York as the shaker pictured left.

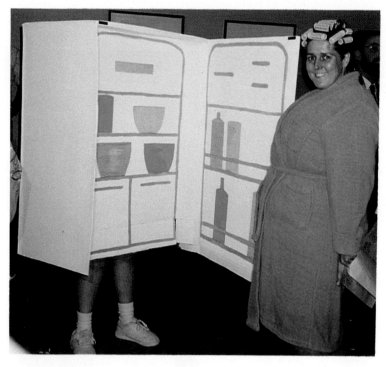

Joan Szoc, as fat lady, and Karen Miller, as refrigerator, both of Massachusetts. Shaker pictured above right.

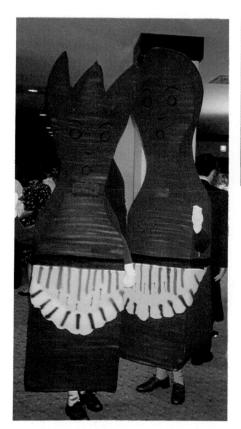

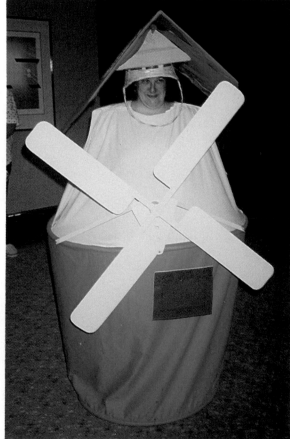

Betsy Reid and Shirley Solomon of New York City as spoon and fork shakers. Shakers pictured above right.

Melissa Werchovsky of Danbury, Connecticut as plastic windmill shaker pictured above. Shakers pictured below left.

Bob and Joyce Gentile from Woodstock, Illinois, as a risque salt and pepper shaker. Shaker pictured above center.

Jan Chappel of Evanston, Illinois as squash head person pictured right.

Andrea Goldberg of Monticello, New York as Humpty Dumpty. Shaker pictured above right.

Jan and David Peters of Venice, California, as Big Boy shakers, pictured at left.

┅┅ Introduction and Acknowledgments ┅┅

This is truly a "Collectors' Book!" After writing three books on salt and pepper shakers, it was no longer feasible to rely on shakers that came through my hands alone to do this fourth book. Therefore I decided to go to some of the best and largest collections of shakers — both to those who specialize, and those whose collections are general; to collectors both in this country and abroad. I hope the resultant book will be as satisfying and exciting to collectors as it has been to me.

I traveled to Memphis, Tennessee, to Stroudsburg, Pennsylvania, and to London, England. I received offers of photographs from Wyoming, Illinois, Connecticut, and New York. The cooperation of collectors has been outstanding.

Dot and J.C. Gammon picked me up at the airport in Memphis, and were wonderful and gracious hosts for my four day visit. Their good friend and photographer, Dianna Crumpler, of Memphis, never lost her patience once in twelve straight hours of shooting. Her good humor and expertise were much appreciated. Dot's collection housed in a two-story barn and in a second "shaker shack," numbers over 15,000 pairs, and from this vast array I selected about 600 pairs to use in the book. Most of the shakers in the section, "Made in America" are from Dot's collection.

As an example of just how many shakers are out there, consider this: I went to Memphis in March of 1992; in June of the same year my husband and I drove to Stroudsburg, Pennsylvania, where we were cordially hosted by Clara and Hubert McHugh. Their collection numbers over 6,000 pairs and I found another 100+ sets that I had never seen before! Every time I tell my own photographer, Michael La Chioma, that this is our last shoot, I find something else wonderful that just *has* to be included.

In February 1992, my husband and I went to England. We had the great good fortune to visit the home of Nigel Dalley in Leamington Spa at the time of a meeting of the British Novelty Salt and Pepper Shakers Club. It was wonderful to meet the British collectors, to learn from them, and to be made an honorary member of their club. But of course the most special part of the day was seeing part of Nigel's fabulous collection of condiment sets, 124 of which are pictured in this book. A million thanks to Nigel for giving me his marvelous slides, and for allowing me to reproduce them here.

Many of the wonderful character and cartoon sets are from the collection of PIN-ON, INC., of Ridgefield, Connecticut. They were photographed by Roman Woloszyn of Beacon Falls, Connecticut. Diane Cauwels, of Tennessee, contributed 60 pairs of black salt and pepper shakers from her collection of Black Americana. They were photographed by Sande Abernathy of Murfreesboro, Tennessee. Joyce Wofford, of Landers, Wyoming also contributed sets from her collection of Black Americana, and they were photographed by Fremont Photography of Landers, Wyoming.

Betsy Zalewski of Pittsburgh, Pennsylvania contributed photographs of nodders and advertising sets from her collection, and they were photographed by Princess Photography Studio in Dormont, Pennsylvania. . .Peter Capell, of Chicago, Illinois, has an extensive collection of gasoline memorabilia. He spoke at the Chicago Salt and Pepper Shaker Convention in 1991, and gave me the slides that he used in his very informative talk there. Dianne Thorn, of Scotrun, Pennsylvania, contributed some wonderful photographs that she took herself of very special nodders and blacks.

Marilyn Di Prima of Illinois sent me a picture of a beautiful swan condiment set that was photographed by Lorraine Haywood. Linda McPherson of Memphis, and Irene Thornburg sent photographs and helped with pricing some of the Ceramic Arts Studio sets. Charlene Wallace of Bridgeport, Connecticut, Rita and Don Longabucco, of Lake Carmel, New York, and Michele Okamoto of Ridgefield, Connecticut, all loaned me shakers that were photographed by the ever faithful and accommodating Michael La Chioma of Hot Shot Studios of Stratford, Connecticut. Thanks also to Steve Justin of Minnesota, and Jean Moon of Illinois for information on their special interests.

A word about pricing. There are still loads of shakers to be found in the $8-$15 range. The sets that are really expensive are the extremely rare and special sets that are obviously hard to find. The collectors who provided photographs of their very special sets also suggested prices. Since they are the ones who have sought out and paid for these sets, and who have acquired a certain expertise in their own speciality, I did use their suggested prices in this book. However, this is still a *guide*; rare shakers can still be found for less, and fairly common shakers will be found for more than the prices in this book. It depends largely on where you buy them — from an antique shop, a flea market, or at a garage sale. Price is also determined by the quantity one purchases — whether a whole collection, or an individual pair. The locale is important too — big city versus small town, etc.

In any case I hope you will enjoy the book as a reference, and an addition to your Collectors' library.

I am eternally grateful to all the people who cared, who trusted me with their precious shakers, and who went out of their way to help make this book possible. Without you, the collectors, this book would never have been written.

DUES - $15 yr US, Canada, Mexico
$20 yr UK, New Zealand, other
FOUR NEWSLETTERS - ANNUAL CONVENTION
Club Information: Irene Thornburg
581 Joy Rd.
Battle Creek, MI 49017
(616) 963-7954

The speakers at the Club Conventions and the articles in the Club Newsletters are both educational and informative. They provide a wonderful way to increase your knowledge about your collection. Aside from all that, the club meetings provide sociability and just plain fun.

Willie & Millie Penguins — Kool Cigarettes.

Top: Big Boy. The old sets, from the 1970s, note difference in checks and hair color. $150.00-200.00.

Center: Big Boy. The new set, 1990's; Big Boy is 5" tall and the hamburger is 2¼" tall. Made in USA from Elias Brothers Restaurants, Inc. $60.00-65.00.

Bottom: Mr. Peanut by Benjamin & Medwin, Inc., 5" tall; made in Taiwan, 1992. $20.00-35.00. This is an older Peanut set, ceramic. $100.00-125.00.

Top: This Elsie and Elmer set of salt and peppers is from the 1940's. $45.00-55.00.

Center: Borden's Elsie and her twins. $100.00-125.00.

Bottom: Another new set — Budman — for Anheuser Busch Budweiser Beer. (Old set has blue shoes) made by Ceramarte in Brazil 1991. 3½" tall. $25.00-35.00. Cloralex Bleach, other side says "free miniature for use as salt shaker." PINOL, pinewood aroma cleanser. Same note on back. $12.00-15.00.

Top: Campbell Kids. The newer set, large range size. $15.00.

Center: Nabisco Blue Bonnet Sue, also by Benjamin & Medwin; discontinued. $25.00-30.00.

Bottom: Campell Soup cans — salt &pepper made for barbecues. $6.00-8.00. New Era potato chip cans. $8.00-10.00.

Top: Red Lobster shakers (may have been "borrowed" from restaurant!) $6.00-8.00. French's pepper and Sterling salt, small picnic size. $6.00-8.00. Burger Chef, $4.00-6.00.

Center: Sprite soda cans. $6.00-8.00. Marathon Mile-Maker gas pumps. $35.00-40.00.

Bottom: Diamond Crystal Shaker salt — cardboard. $8.00-10.00. Inlet Valley Farms, Inc. $25.00-30.00. Seagram's 7-Crown, these were given to me by Bobbie Segal at Brimfield, Massachusetts. Bobbie is a salt and pepper shaker dealer and club member. $25.00-30.00.

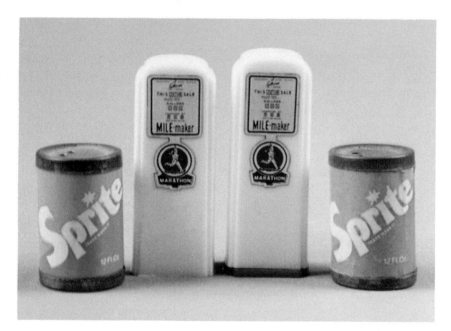

Top: Bill's Beer Miniatures in original box — three sets of mugs. $18.00-24.00. Stroh's beer bottles. The older sets have metal caps — these would also appeal to beer collectors. $12.00-15.00.

Center Left: Evinrude motors — these are very nice and quite unusual. They were given to employees for Christmas. $125.00-150.00. Contributed by Marty Grossman, NY.

Bottom Left: Kentucky Colonel Harlan Sanders, left is a single bust; his mate is missing. She is Mrs. Sanders. 3½" tall soft plastic; marked "Marquardt Corp. 1972." $40.00-45.00. Full figure, hard plastic in original package. Back of package is written in French; 1965 — marked "Starling Plastics Ltd. London, Canada." These are 4¼" tall. $65.00-75.00.

Bottom Right: Hamm's Beer, ceramic; one shaker pours from the top of his head; the other from his nose. 5" tall; Ceramarte, Brazil, $125.00-150.00.

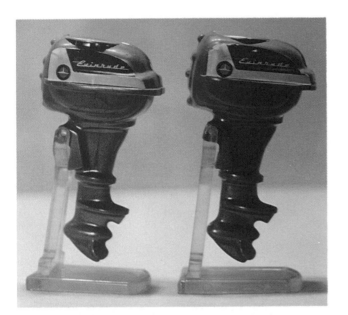

Top: Philgas tanks. $30.00-35.00.
Firestone Tires. $40.00-50.00.

Gas pump shakers were first introduced in the 1950's; they are 2½" tall and were made in the exact colors and adorned with decals or labels of most brands of the 50's and 60's. They were a promotional giveaway by service stations. National and regional brands such as Phillips 66, Esso, and Texaco are most abundant. Local brands such as Apco in Iowa, Clark in Illinois, Zephyr and Leonard in Michigan, Signal and Hancock in California, and Keystone and United in Pennsylvania are much harder to find. Originally, sets were boxed individually; later they were packaged in bulk. Peter Capell, who supplied this information, and the following slides, is seeking rare sets; he currently owns 73 different sets, and is looking for: Agway, APCO, Ashland, Bay, Calso, Derby, Dixie, El Paso, Fleet Wing, FS, Hancock, Hudson, Husky, Imperial Refineries, Martin, MFA, Shamrock, Signal, SOC, Tenneco, Total, Vickers, Zephyr. If any of these are found, please contact the author through Collector Books.

Center: Sinclair changed the name of the additive in its Power-X gas and the two varieties are shown here. The only variation is the small decal below the meter. $45.00-50.00.

Bottom: Amoco, green and yellow — regional color variety; both date from same period, mid to late 1950's. Red is another color available. $45.00-55.00.

Top: Shell had three varieties over two decades beginning with the plain set, then with the "new" TCP additive, then with the more modern colors and pump design. Earliest from 1950's. $35.00. Latest from early 1970's. $45.00.

Center: ESSO is the second most commonly found, as not only Standard of New Jersey gave them away, but the same were given by the Canadian operation, the Imperial Oil Company. These are from the 1960's as are the Texaco shakers. $35.00-45.00.

Bottom: Cities Service, at one time a national marketer, had variations reflecting the modernization of their gas pumps and graphics from the early 1950's through the 1970's. $45.00-55.00.

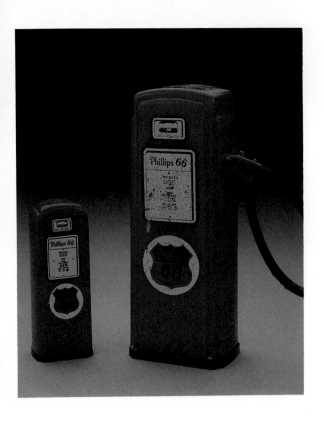

Left: Phillips 66 shows the gas pump shaker (small) and the bank (large); Several companies also gave away banks as promotional item in late 50's and 60's. Bank, $25.00+. S&P, $20.00-30.00.

Right: Blue Sunoco reflects 1950-60 brand identity of the Sun Oil Company. $40.00-50.00.

Bottom: Texaco was apparently more creative with its promotional use of the gas pump salt &pepper and had a Christmas box designed to replace its plain logo version. $25.00-35.00. In box, $45.00.

Top: Standard Oil of Indiana evolved from the plain red of the 1950's to the more colorful version of the early 1960's, and added a crown shown here. Ironically, the original colorful pumps were crownless; the actual crowns were tire air hose caps and were added to the salt &pepper later. $35.00-45.00.

Center: These ceramic gas pumps are English and were a gift; made in the 1980's. Maker unknown. $20.00-25.00.

Bottom: Mobilgas ceramic shield shaped salt and pepper (holes on each end.) Peter Capell only knows of four of these, all from the same gas station in Nebraska. Early 1950's. $50.00.

Animals

Dinosaurs

Top: Cartoon tigers. $10.00-12.00. Luster black cats. $15.00-18.00.

Center: Cats with rhinestone eyes. $25.00-30.00.

Bottom Left: Cat with foot through basket — a marvel that these survived! $15.00-18.00. Knock off Donald Ducks — these are not Disney. $15.00-18.00.

Bottom Right: Cool cat sitting on a block of ice. $18.00-22.00.

Top: Cats and elephants — these are German, and very appealing. $25.00-30.00 per pair.

Center: Black and white scotties. $8.00-10.00. Stylized horses. $6.00-8.00.

Bottom: Rabbits and dogs — solid color — German. $35.00-40.00.

Top: Dog heads in shoe — PY Japan. $25.00-30.00. Poodle heads in basket. $18.00-20.00.

Center: Collies — nice quality, and realistic. $25.00-35.00.

Bottom: Beautiful realistic boxers. $35.00-40.00. Pointers. $35.00-40.00.

Top: Basset hounds and English bulldogs — both great. $35.00-45.00 per pair.

Upper Center: Deer and goats. $22.00-26.00.

Lower Center: Dalmatians and greyhounds. $22.00-26.00.

Bottom: Calves and ponies — bone china. $22.00-26.00.

Top: More bone china animals: antelope, bear, and elephants. $22.00-26.00 per pair.

Upper Center: Bone china horses, calves and goats. $22.00-26.00.

Lower Center: Three different sets of bone china poodles. $22.00-26.00.

Bottom: Hippos, ram and ewe, and donkeys. $22.00-26.00.

Top Left: One-piece rocking bears. $22.00-24.00.

Top Right: Cartoon type cows. $8.00-10.00.

Upper Center: Zebra and foxes. $10.00-12.00.

Lower Center: Dogs. $18.00-22.00.

Bottom: Bone china rabbits, moose, pig, and deer. $20.00-22.00.

Top: Cartoon type gorillas in cage. $10.00-15.00.

Upper Center: One-piece skunk. $8.00-10.00. One-piece bunnies. $12.00-18.00.

Lower Center: Hugging bunnies. $8.00-10.00. Monkeys. $8.00-10.00.

Bottom: Monkey see no evil, hear no evil and speak no evil. $15.00-18.00. Monkey and telephone. $15.00-18.00.

Top: Mother and baby bear. $15.00-18.00. PY Dr. dog and patient. $25.00-30.00.

Center: Giraffe heads. $15.00-18.00. Horse heads. $15.00-18.00.

Bottom: These three sets are part of a series — I would be interested to know if anyone has any others. The mouse and the bowling ball fit together with a triangle — indented in the mouse, raised on the ball (or vice versa). They are precarious, but do fit! $18.00-24.00 per pair.

Top: Frog and toadstool. $6.00-8.00. Frogs playing leapfrog. $10.00-12.00.

Center: Camel – Enesco. $20.00-22.00. Sphinx — a one-piece shaker. $20.00-22.00.

Bottom: Hippos. $8.00-10.00. Armadillo — this is a single, but the only one I've ever seen and I actually know someone who collects them (armadillos)! $10.00.

Top: Dinosaurs with twisted necks — these are wonderful and amazingly not chipped or broken. $25.00-30.00. Dinosaurs. $20.00-25.00.

Upper Center: Elephant carrier. $10.00-12.00. One-piece cow. $10.00-12.00.

Lower Center: One-piece dog and doghouse — each has cork. $10.00-15.00. Pigs (?) in a doghouse. $8.00-10.00.

Bottom: Two more pairs of dinosaurs — these are very popular. $15.00-20.00.

Top: These animals look like jointed toys; I love them, although I don't quite know why. Giraffes and dachshunds. $15.00-18.00.

Upper Center: Zebras and circus horses. $15.00-18.00.

Lower Center: Roosters and lions. $15.00-18.00.

Bottom: Horses — jointed and realistic. $15.00-18.00.

Top Left: Each of these cow ladies carries a parasol — most precarious. $25.00-35.00.

Top Right: These are circus sets — upside down performing animals. $25.00-35.00.

Center: Another animal on a drum with a musical performing pair. "Dressed animals" is another whole category of collecting. $18.00-22.00.

Bottom: Charming Deco dogs — wonderful colors. $15.00-18.00. Dressed mice. $10.00-12.00.

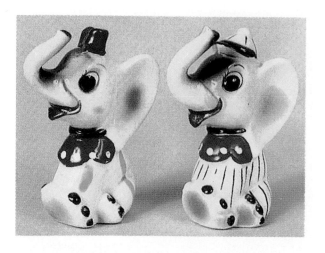

Top Left: Elephants dressed for the circus. $10.00-12.00.

Top Right: Mouse with foot through shoe. $15.00-18.00. Mother and baby set (kangaroos). $15.00-18.00.

Upper Center: Monkeys are German. $25.00-30.00. Elephants in overalls. $10.00-12.00.

These sets are relatively new; they are bone china and all come with trays.

Lower Center: Frogs and rabbits. $8.00-10.00.

Bottom: Elephants and snails. $8.00-10.00.

Top: Frogs and more snails. $8.00-10.00.

Upper Center: Alligators in hats. $6.00-8.00. Donkeys with headbands. $6.00-8.00.

Lower Center: Dressed bunnies and musical rabbits. $10.00-12.00.

Bottom: Dogs and pigs — all dressed up. $15.00-18.00.

These "fuzzies" on these two pages were first collected by Norma Montaigne of Vermont, and I don't really know anyone else who collects them; but somehow when you see a bunch of them together, they begin to have a certain charm. $5.00-8.00 per pair. Unless they catch on!

Top: Children's animals. $15.00-18.00.

Upper Center: Green-faced monster dogs. $8.00-10.00. Monkeys dressed in clothes. $20.00-22.00.

Lower Center: Pigs in hats and pigs in pants. $10.00-14.00.

Bottom Left: Tropical monkeys. $15.00-18.00. Alligators in people shirts — a switch! $10.00-12.00.

Bottom Right: Dressed cartoon dogs. $10.00-12.00.

Top Left: The dogs on the barstool are marked Enesco — "the bar-hounds," and are part of a series. $24.00-28.00.

Top Right: Dressed dog couples. $15.00-18.00.

Center: These goats are on the same type green ball as the Zodiac fish — but there are no zodiac signs; another series, perhaps? $18.00-22.00. A wonderful goat with bag — similar to the doctor goat and the barber goat. $28.00-32.00.

Bottom: Penguins with umbrellas, and ducks with bonnets. $18.00-20.00.

Top Left: Teddy Bear Swinger (stand is one shaker and bear on swing is another). $15.00-18.00.

Top Right: A wonderful pair of elephants on an elephant tray. $45.00-50.00.

Upper Center: Rabbits on motorcycles with headbands to hold back their ears — of course! $20.00-25.00. Stylized yellow rabbits. $10.00-12.00.

Lower Center: Political animals — two-piece shakers Democrat and Republican. $40.00-50.00 per pair.

Bottom: Hare and tortoise in a boat. $10.00-12.00. Another pair of animals that look like toy ducks. $15.00-18.00.

⟶ American Made Shakers ⟶

This section is about shakers that were made in the United States. Several companies flourished in the 1940's. At the time that the United States entered World War II, imports were drastically curtailed, and the demand for American made products increased dramatically.

Ceramic Arts Studio was founded in Madison, Wisconsin in 1941 by Lawrence Rabbitt and Rueben Sand. The following year Betty Harrington came to the pottery, and began to create figurines. A German craftsman, Otto Longhammer, made the molds. Sand took these early figurines to Marshall Field & Co. in Chicago, and sales were immediate. By 1943, increased demand and production necessitated the hiring of many more workers. One notable applicant was a musician named Zona Liberace. She was married to the famed pianist's father! Lee Liberace was a frequent visitor to the plant, and Betty Harrington once made him a copy of his famous gold piano complete with a tiny Liberace seated on a stool. For many years Zona Liberace was head decorator at the studio. Betty Harrington designed over 460 models of figurines; a young German named "Ullie" specialized in animals. The peak year for CAS was 1945–6 when 350,000–450,000 pieces were made per year and the company employed 100 persons. After 1950 Japanese imports threatened the American ceramics industry, and by 1955 Ceramic Arts Studio shut down.[1] There were Japanese copies of several CAS salt and pepper sets. Those I have seen include the mother and baby polar bear, the red and white clown and dog, and the small Oriental and Dutch couples.

Rosemeade was made by the Whapeton Pottery Company which opened in 1940 in Whapeton, North Dakota. The factory closed in the early 1960's. The clay came from Mandau, North Dakota. The name Rosemeade came from owner Laura Taylor Hughes' childhood home in Rosemeade Township in Ransom County. Most pieces of the pottery have a paper sticker with the name of a wild prairie rose, a flower native to the state. Some pieces were marked with the name Rosemeade in black or blue lettering on the bottom, and a few rare pieces were marked Anne K., one of the painters at the pottery. If the paper label is gone, identification can be made by becoming familiar with the unique softly shaded coloration and the semi–matte finish of the glazes.[2]

Triangle Studios/Vallona Star Ceramics. This company was listed in Los Angeles, California in 1945 and 1948. By 1949 they were in El Monte, California. Owners were Valeria de Marsa and Everett S. Frost. Ebeling and Reuss, Inc. were distributors. In 1945 Vallona Star was listed as a trade name for the art pottery of the Triangle Studios. By 1954, the pottery was no longer listed.[3]

Some photographs contributed by Irene Thornburg of Michigan.

[1]*Harrington Figurines*, Sabra Olson Laumbach, 1985. Ferguson Communications, Hillsdale, MI. pp.4–12.
[2]*Beautiful Rosemeade*, Shirley Sampson & Irene Harms, Sanders Printing Co. 1986.
[3]*Lehner's Encyclopedia of U.S. Marks on Pottery, Porcelain, and Clay*, 1988, Lois Lehner.

Top Left: Boy and girl "Lover boy and willing." $90.00-110.00.

Top Right: Kangaroos and babies. $75.00-85.00.

Center: Giraffes — yellow and green. $90.00-110.00.

Bottom: Parrots and Roosters. The parrot's names are Budgie and Pudgie. $65.00-75.00.

Top Left: Girl and boy on chairs (two pairs). $75.00-95.00 pair.

Top Right: Stylized cats. $65.00-70.00. Mother and baby skunk. $45.00-55.00.

Center: Elephants "Tembo," 6½" and "Tembino," 2½". $115.00-125.00.

Bottom: Donkey and elephant; mother and baby bear. $75.00-85.00.

Top: Lions and Leopards. $95.00-105.00.

Left Center: Donkeys. $40.00-45.00.

Right Center: Sultan and harem girl. $95.00-110.00.

Bottom Left: Stylized mother, 4" and baby deer, 2¼". $85.00-95.00.

Bottom Right: Brown camels. $115.00-125.00.

Top Left: Minehaha and Hiawatha, 6½" and 4½". $150.00-165.00.

Top Right: Fox and goose. $60.00-75.00.

Upper Center: Clown and dog. $60.00-70.00. Horse heads. $45.00-55.00.

Lower Center: Rabbits. $40.00-45.00.

Bottom: Elf and toadstool, frog and toadstool. $50.00-60.00.

Top: Spanish dancing couple, 7½" tall. $100.00-125.00.

Upper Center: Zebras. $115.00-125.00.

Lower Center: Calico cat and gingham dog; cat and creamer. $50.00-75.00.

Bottom: Poodle in pillow, Boxer dogs, stylized lambs. $35.00-45.00.

Top Left: Chinese couple and "Wee" French couple. $25.00-35.00.

Top Right: Tall gypsy couple. $110.00-125.00.

►•► Rosemeade

Center: Bulldog heads. $45.00-50.00. Standing dogs. $30.00-40.00. Donkey heads. $30.00-35.00.

Bottom: Skunks — two sizes. $40.00-45.00.

Top: Cacti. $40.00-50.00.

Upper Center: Pheasants, quail, and deer. These are the most common. $30.00-35.00.

Lower Center: Pink pelicans and sailboats. $40.00-50.00.

Bottom: Flamingos. $50.00-60.00. Swordfish (rare). $100.00-125.00.

Top: Corn on corn shaped tray and standing ground hogs. $35.00-45.00 per pair.

Upper Center: Chihuahua heads. $75.00-100.00. Palomino horse heads. $60.00-70.00.

Lower Center: Dog heads. $40.00-50.00 per pair.

Bottom Left: Running rabbits. $35.00-45.00.

Bottom Right: Birds — blue birds and robins. $45.00-55.00.

Top: Bears. $45.00-55.00.

Center: Reddish Bears and Elephants. $45.00-50.00.

Bottom: Fish. These are very realistic and make a beautiful grouping. $40.00-50.00 per pair.

Poinsetta Studio

Little is known about this pottery except that it was made in California, has very nice quality glazes, and is usually trimmed in gold.

Top Left: Two-piece lamp and Mr. and Mrs. Santa. $25.00-30.00.

Top Right: Skunk and flower. $25.00-30.00. Seated black couple. $45.00-50.00.

Upper Center: Circus horse and wagon and train. $25.00-30.00.

Lower Center: Hare and tortoise and boy with candle and clock. $18.00-25.00.

Bottom Left: Striking black and yellow fish on tray and bird on stump. $18.00-25.00.

Bottom Right: Genie and lamp and toadstool and elf. $18.00-25.00.

Top Left: Lamps on stand trimmed with typical flowers and gold. $18.00-22.00.

Top Right: Cowboy and girl with wagon wheel as tray. $30.00-35.00.

Upper Center: Ducks on tray with plastic reeds; I have this set with the gold Poinsetta label on the bottom, and also one marked "Made in Japan." The Japanese set did not have the gold trim. $30.00-35.00.

Lower Center: Bride's cookbook and The way to his Heart (also in Japanese version). Teapot on trivet. $18.00-22.00.

Bottom: Cats on tray and flowers in basket. $18.00-25.00.

Sorcha Boru

Sorcha Boru was the professional name used by Claire Stewart, a ceramicist from California. She was one of the founders of the Allied Arts Guild of Menlo Park. She had a studio there from 1932-38. She then operated Sorcha Boru Ceramics in San Carlos until 1955. She made slip-decorated figures, most of which were incised S.B.C. by hand.[1] I think these are very charming — almost primitive.

Top Left: Two sets of children. $50.00-60.00.

Top Right: Bride and groom. $75.00-85.00.

Bottom: Sailor boy on wave and girl. $75.00-80.00. Two children. $40.00-50.00.

[1]*Schroeder's Antique Price Guide.* Tenth Edition, 1992. Collector Books. P.65.

Top: Little Miss Muffet, and the hare and the tortoise. $40.00-50.00 per pair.

Upper Center: Drip and Drop and daisies. There are many Japanese versions of Drip and Drop. $25.00-30.00.

Lower Center: Indian and corn. $35.00-40.00. White kittens. $25.00-30.00.

Bottom Left: Vegetable heads trimmed in gold. $40.00-50.00.

Bottom Right: Spaceship and creature. $50.00-60.00.

Birds, Fish, and Fowl

Top: These ducks almost look like wood but they are ceramic. $8.00-10.00. Platypus (?). $8.00-10.00.

Upper Center: Funny fish and mermaid and star fish. $10.00-12.00.

Lower Center: These fish with people faces are another example of anthropomorphic shakers. $15.00-18.00.

Bottom Left: Dressed up fish — a lovely couple from Miami Beach. $8.00-10.00.

Bottom Right: Standing fish — part of a series — all have same green base. $20.00-24.00. Funny penguins with silver feet — salt comes out of holes in eyes. $10.00-12.00.

Top: Spotted fish — rainbow trout; yellow perch. $25.00-35.00.

Upper Center: These realistic fish are by Enesco. Gray with white spots — Northern Pike; all gray — pickerel. $25.00-35.00.

Lower Center: Long blue fish. $25.00-35.00. Luster toucans. $25.00-35.00.

Bottom: Polka dot children's face fish and realistic rainbow trout. $25.00-35.00.

Top Left: Birds on baskets. S&P's are the eggs. $12.00-15.00.

Top Right: Very nicely colored birds. $15.00-18.00.

Upper Center: Birds on baskets. $12.00-15.00.

Lower Center: Two pairs of seals, marked New England Ceramics made in Torrington, Ct. $10.00-12.00.

Bottom: The pair of birds on the left are made in Germany. $40.00-45.00. The large toucans on the right are English, and are the Guiness toucans. $75.00-85.00.

Top Left: The mermaids on the left are by Norcrest; both sets. $18.00-22.00.

Top Right: These pelicans are very heavy metal, and beautifully detailed. $40.00-45.00.

Upper Center: Mermaids are very collectible; the four by Enesco say "Long time no he, and Long time no she" across the bottom. $18.00-22.00.

Lower Center: German toucans and comic blue birds. $25.00-35.00.

Bottom: A cock fight — the center rooster is for toothpicks. $15.00-18.00. Very striking black and white chickens. $14.00-16.00.

Character Sets

This category is among the most collectible, and the most expensive. The really early sets (1930's) are extremely hard to find. Besides appealing to salt and pepper shaker collectors, these are very desirable to Disney and other cartoon collectors.

Top: Mickey Mouse in chair and Mickey Mouse in the car were made by the Good Co., a division of Applause, Inc. They were made in Korea in 1989, and are marked "The Walt Disney Company." $25.00-30.00.

Upper Center: Donald and the salt mines is in a box marked "Mickey and Pals," also the Good Co. These newer sets are still available and so still inexpensive. $15.00-20.00.

Lower Center: Mickey Mouse Condiment set — early 1930's; very rare. $500.00+. Another early set from the 1930's. $250.00-300.00.

Bottom: Felix the cat — small set 1930's. $100.00-125.00. Shmoos — immortalized by Al Capp. 1940's. $175.00-200.00.

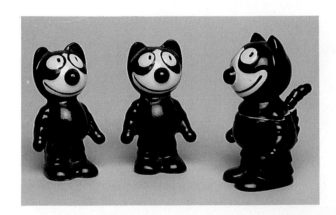

Top: Felix the cat condiment set — the spoon is his tail. Japan, 1930. $400.00+.

Upper Center: Popeye condiment set luster; Japanese; very rare. $400.00+.

Lower Center: Skunk 1940, full bee, Goebel, Walt Disney (marked WDP) — boys have no eyelashes. Character is Flower. $125.00-150.00.

Bottom: Thumper — full bee mark by Goebel. $125.00-150.00. Fantasia mushrooms by Vernon Kiln, USA — Disney copyright 1941. $200.00-225.00.

Top: Moon Mullins. $25.00-35.00. Moon Mullins black face. $35.00-45.00.

Upper Center: Variations of Smokey the Bear — large set; heads only. $25.00-35.00.

Lower Center: Ferdinand the bull and Figaro the cat from Pinocchio (unmarked). $35.00-45.00.

Bottom: Three little pigs. $35.00-45.00. Two smaller pigs. $20.00-30.00. All marked Japan.

Top: Smokey the Bear condiment set – rare. Japan, 1950's. $120.00-160.00.

Center and Bottom: Snow White boxed set. Japan, 1950's. $160.00-180.00.

Top and Upper Center: Five of the Seven Dwarfs — marked foreign — usually means Japan. $100.00-125.00 pair.

Bottom Left and Right: This set of Dwarfs is marked Walt Disney Co. and also has a Japanese mark on the bottom. They are from Disneyland, Japan. $110.00-125.00.

Top: Glass depression era Mickey Mouse set — red and yellow plastic tops — rare; from the 1930's. $250.00-300.00.

Left Center: The Mickey Christmas sets are Disney, Japan. $35.00-45.00.

Right Center: Two seated dwarfs. 1930's Wade Heath. Walt Disney — Snow White Dwarfs — English. $450.00-650.00.

Bottom: Snow White with Doc and Dopey — Snow White is a napkin holder. $300.00+.

Top: Plastic Mickeys are from 1972 — made for Wilton, Inc., Chicago marked Walt Disney Production in Hong Kong. $25.00-35.00. Pinocchio set. $45.00-55.00.

Center: Woody Woodpecker and his girlfriend — Walter Lanz 1990; cold paint (these were on ABC Television coverage of The Vermont Convention and sold at auction for $95.00. $45.00-65.00. Mickey Chef — "The Walt Disney Co." by Hoan, Ltd. Made in Taiwan. $20.00-25.00.

Bottom: These large all white Mickey heads are made in the U.S. $20.00-25.00.

Top: Mickey Mouse Club hats and Alice in Wonderland set — new. $18.00-25.00.

Upper Center: Mickey and Pluto and Mickey and Minnie Christmas also newer. $35.00-45.00.

Lower Center: Mickey as Santa in sled and Goofy and Donald. $50.00-60.00.

Bottom: Mother, Goose, and House on tray. Japan, 1950-60. $80.00-120.00.

Top: This is a wonderful set of a popular Japanese cartoon called Astro Boy. This set represents Astro Boy and his sister in a rocket. $150.00-175.00.

Center: Betty Boop napkin holder, salt and pepper combination by Vandor. $90.00-110.00.

Bottom: Two sets of the ever popular cartoon cat Garfield. Left $80.00-90.00; right $25.00-30.00.

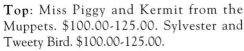

Top: Miss Piggy and Kermit from the Muppets. $100.00-125.00. Sylvester and Tweety Bird. $100.00-125.00.

Upper Center and Lower Left Center: Two of these Walter Lanz characters from the 1950's appeared in my third book. They were Woody and Winnie. Here are Knothead and Splinter, Andy and Miranda, Wally, Windy, Willie, and Homer. $75.00-85.00.

Lower Right Center: "Cereal Sisters" were introduced at Epcot Center in Walt Disney World. They were part of the Kraft Kitchen Krackpots and were Andrew Sisters sound–alikes. Miss Oats is pink and Miss Corn is yellow (1981-$8.50). $65.00-75.00-1992.

Bottom Left: Fred Flintstone and Wilma by Vandor; discontinued 1991. $75.00-85.00. Tasmanian Devil by Warner Bros. $30.00-35.00.

Bottom Right: Cracker Jack sailors — glass, 1930's. $45.00-55.00.

Top: Mammy and Pappy Yokum, characters by Al Capp. $200.00-250.00.

Upper Center: Here are two chalkware comic sets from the 1940's, Barney Google and Snuffy Smith, and Sad Sack. ©George Baker. Norcrest Label. $200.00+.

Lower Center: Two wonderful Pinocchio sets. The one on the left is with Jiminy Cricket/ the other set is a condiment set. This set was bought by a U.S. soldier after WWII in Occupied Japan in 1946. The McHughs bought the set from that soldier. Pinocchio is the salt, Jiminy Cricket is the pepper and the house is the mustard. Pinocchio and Jiminy Cricket alone. $100.00-125.00. The condiment set, very rare. $400.00+.

Bottom: Two different sets of Maggie and Jiggs, and an unusual pair of outhouses marked with their names. The figures, $175.00-200.00; the outhouses, $35.00-45.00.

Top: This is a short fat Popeye and with him Olive Oyl. $150.00-175.00. Charlie McCarthy. $125.00-150.00.

Upper Center: Daisy and bag of groceries, and Pluto and doghouse; both sets are new. $18.00-22.00.

Lower Center: Raggedy Ann, the beloved character developed by Johnny Gruelle in 1918 is having her 75th birthday! There are now many objects made besides the rag doll; here, Ann and Andy cookie jars with a pair of plastic salt and pepper shakers. The shakers, $15.00-18.00.

Bottom: Two more Raggedy Ann and Andy salt and pepper shakers — ceramic. $22.00-25.00.

Top: Variations on a theme: An unusual Raggedy Ann and Andy. $28.00-32.00. Two dolls that may or may not be Raggedy, her clothes aren't right and, of course, there's no Andy. $12.00-15.00.

Upper Center: According to Melva Davern's book II, this series is by Arcadia of California — I'm so glad she found a paper sticker on one! Mary and her lamb and Peter and his wife. $35.00-40.00.

Lower Center: Little Miss Muffet and the Spider — and The Old Lady in the Shoe. $35.00-40.00.

Bottom: A King and Queen and dish and spoon. $25.00-30.00.

Top: These are from another series: Mary, Lamb, Peter and his wife. $25.00-30.00.

Upper Center: Two very unusual sets of Red Riding Hood and the Wolf. $45.00-50.00 per pair.

Lower Center: Lady and the Tramp — a new set sold at Walt Disney World is part of a dinnerware set from Tony's Cafe. From the movie: Lady and the Tramp, 2¾" tall. $20.00-25.00. Huey, Dewey, or Louey — chalkware sets, 2¾" tall. Holes are in ducks' tails. ©Walt Disney on base in back of shakers. $35.00-45.00.

Bottom Left: Paul Bunyan and his Blue Ox, Babe. Marked G. Nov. Co. Japan. $35.00-40.00.

Bottom Right: Little Jack Horner on a cushion. $22.00-25.00. Alice in Wonderland and the Caterpillar. $30.00-35.00.

Top: Two wonderful sets of Humpty Dumpty. The painter and letter carrier Norcrest. H. 714. $40.00-45.00.

Upper Center: Jungle Book set; lightweight ceramic; stamped on base of both shakers Co. MCMLXIV Walt Disney Productions written in fancy lettering. Sticker is shape of cat in silver; says: Calaco Imports, Japan. Elephant 3½" tall; Mowgli 4¾" tall. $180.00-200.00. Ludwig Von Drake; both stamped WD-33 1961..also has sticker that says Dan Brechner exclusive, New York 10, N.Y Japan; cold paint. $125.00-150.00.

Lower Center: Popeye and Olive Oyl newer unauthorized set, bisque type material. $30.00-40.00. Ziggy and his dog by Tom Wilson. Sticker on bottom says Ziggy tm Universal Press Syndicate MCMLXXIX WWA Inc. Cleveland. Made in Japan. Eyes in both holes for salt and pepper. 2" and 2¾" tall. $30.00-35.00.

Bottom: Three Little Pigs Condiment Set. $60.00-75.00. The Owl and The Pussycat by Fitz and Floyd. 1980. $80.00-120.00.

Top Left: Black and white Mickey condiment set German. $400.00+.

Top Right: This is an incredible German set from the 1930's when Mickey was black and white and had a very pointy nose. These are baby Mickeys looking up from their carriage at their cat nurse. $400.00+.

Center: Black and white Mickey Mouse condiment set; center mouse has black hands. This set is also German, but from the 1920's. I saw this set (or very similar) at the Atlantic City Antique Show three years ago. It was $1500.00, but the owner said that since I was a dealer, I could have it for $1200.00! I'm grateful to Nigel Dalley for allowing me to show his slides here, and picture this rare set. $1200.00-1600.00.

Bottom: Peter Peter Pumpkin Eater. 1950-60. $80.00-120.00.

Condiment Sets

Animals

Top: Cats and goldfish bowl. Note the spoon handle is a fish. $95.00-110.00.

Center: This set of dogs might have had a tray; the mustard pot is a football and the spoon handle is a dog's head. It is miraculous that these tiny china spoons survived. $95.00-110.00.

Bottom: Three black cats and a ball of yarn — the spoon handle is the cat's head. The tray for this, according to Rich O'Donnell, is in the form of a braided rug. $200.00+ with tray.

Top Left and Center: Two stacking pig sets; the yellow one seems of finer quality. Better detail to face and shoes. $70.00-75.00.

Top Right: Dogs — a different style; I have seen these dogs many times as just salt and pepper shakers, and had no idea that they were part of a condiment set — and toothpick holder. $65.00-75.00.

Bottom Left: Bears — but why a lobster claw on the mustard? $85.00-90.00.

Bottom Right: More of the same series: kangaroos; this spoon looks like one of the boxing gloves. $85.00-90.00.

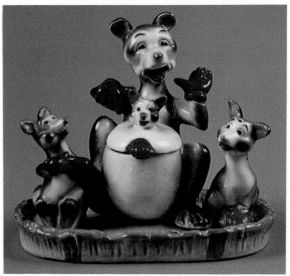

Top Left: Three white Bonzo type dogs on tray — German. $175.00-200.00.

Top Right: German dogs with radio headphones. 1930's. $100.00-120.00.

Center: The three little pigs with house. Japan, 1950-60. $250.00-275.00.

Bottom Left: Rabbits with cabbage. Japan, 1960's. $85.00-110.00.

Bottom Right: Two dogs on heart-shaped box. Japan, 1930's. $90.00-100.00.

Top Left: Three black and white rabbits by Grafton. English. $150.00-175.00.

Top Right: Elephant with Eastern man on top — man is the lid to the mustard and the flower baskets on sides are the salt and pepper. Japan, 1950's. $100.00-140.00.

Center: Three white dogs with black and red trim. German, 1920. $110.00-130.00.

Bottom Left: Three different color dogs on tray — unknown. $85.00-100.00.

Bottom Right: Two dogs rowing a boat with a cat in the middle. German, 1930. $175.00-200.00.

Top: Pussy Cat, Pussy Cat where have you been? condiment. 1950-60. $120.00-150.00.

Upper Center: Three monkeys on tray — "see no evil, speak no evil, hear no evil." The tray says "the three wise monkeys." Japan, 1950. $80.00-120.00.

Lower Center: Two frogs on a tray with red flower for mustard. Japan, 1950's. $60.00-80.00.

Bottom: Two-headed red cow — mustard in the middle. German, 1930's. $110.00-125.00.

Top: Dog pulling cart with two barrels — German nodder, 1890's. $140.00-160.00.

Center: Two yellow Bonzo dogs; larger red dog in the middle has a pipe for the spoon and is the mustard. German, 1930's. $175.00-200.00.

Bottom Left: Humpty Dumpty condiment set. Japan, 1950's-60's. $125.00-175.00.

Bottom Right: A wonderfully ugly pig with two pumpkins. German, 1930's. $125.00-150.00.

Top: Elfin people. $50.00-75.00. Three Bonzo dogs — tongue is spoon. $90.00-100.00.

Center: Two more frogs with flower, Japanese. $45.00-50.00. Two Irish men with pot o' gold on a shamrock tray. $50.00-65.00.

➤ Birds, Fish, and Fowl ◄

Bottom: Both chickens are the shakers and the house is the mustard. $35.00-45.00. Bird on a nest with two hanging apples; both these sets are from Japan. $30.00-40.00.

Top: Two more sets; a bird and chickens on a tray. $40.00-45.00.

Upper Center: Beautifully colored duck condiment set. $95.00-100.00. Mother hen and two baby chicks. $45.00-55.00.

Lower Center: This is a beautiful set; the photograph was taken by Lorraine Haywood and the set is owned by Marilyn di Prima. The swan's head and neck are the spoon. $95.00-110.00.

Bottom: The same duck set in luster in much softer colors. $95.00-110.00.

Top: Two sets of lobsters. The set on the yellow tray has bottoms that screw off. $65.00-75.00 each set.

Center: Chicken, rooster, and nest for mustard. Japan Nodder, 1950. $60.00-80.00.

Bottom Left: These lobsters seem to be hanging on heads of lettuce. Japan. $40.00-50.00.

Bottom Right: Two owls with dish for mustard. German, 1890-1907. $80.00-120.00.

Top Left: Yellow duck and two ducklings. German, 1920-30. $120.00-140.00.

Top Right: Owl on branch with two open dishes for salt and pepper, and covered jar for mustard. German, 1910-30. $90.00-100.00.

Center: Black and white fish. English, 1950. $80.00-90.00.

Bottom: Loch-Ness monster. English, 1970. $80.00-90.00.

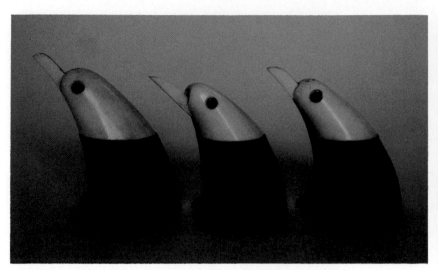

Top Left: Three bakelite penguins — I had bought these in England just as a salt and pepper, and never knew that there was a mustard to match. English, 1930's. $90.00-100.00.

Top Right: Owl and skunk on tree branch. Japan, 1950's. (Strange Combination!) $70.00-90.00.

⊷ Houses and Transportation

Bottom: House, windmill, and well. Made in England by Crown Devon; incised #319. Large house says "Salt Box Inn." $70.00-90.00.

Top: Log cabin with two pine trees. $75.00-85.00.

Upper Center: House with water wheel. $50.00-65.00. Simulated teapot, creamer and sugar; these are the cottage design. $65.00-75.00.

Lower Center: Girl and boy on either side of house; great proportion! $45.00-65.00.

Bottom: Donkey pulling cart. $30.00-40.00. Outhouses with hillbilly lying in front of lamppost. $30.00-40.00.

Top: Horse pulling cart with milk cans. German. $80.00-100.00.

Center: Beautiful carriage — raised work in gold leaf. $75.00-90.00.

Bottom: Two horses pulling green carriage. Japan, 1950's. $80.00-100.00.

Top: Three-part house. German, 1920. $120.00-140.00.

Center: British telephone booth and mailboxes; made in Japan, 1950. $100.00-125.00.

Bottom Left: Lighthouse; two drawers pull out for salt and pepper. German, 1920's. $80.00-120.00.

Bottom Right: Fort and two cannons. Japan, 1950. $80.00-100.00.

Top: Three-piece train. Japan, 1950's. $60.00-80.00.

➤➤➤ International People

Center: Dutch woman and children on tray. $75.00-95.00.

Bottom: Two Oriental men in rocking stand. Japan, 1950's. $65.00-80.00.

Top: Welsh ladies. German, 1920-30. $70.00-100.00.

Center: Two Arabs with camel. Japan, 1950's. $80.00-100.00.

Bottom: Irish couple. German, 1930's. $60.00-90.00.

Chefs

Top: Winking chef with spoon and two pots. Goebel. M-31. German. $120.00-160.00.

Center: Three chefs. German, 1920-30. $80.00-120.00.

Bottom Left: Chef holding a basket. Japan, 1950's. $85.00-95.00.

Bottom Right: Gold and white chef on a pedestal with open salt and pepper. Germany, 1910-30. $150.00-175.00.

Top Left: Chef behind two pumpkins — open salt. German, 1920-30. $125.00-175.00.

Top Right: Chef with two covered pots on a brick oven. Japan. $125.00-150.00.

Sailors

Bottom Left: Beautiful German set — sailor carrying two ships. $80.00-120.00. Unusual navy and white set. $40.00-50.00.

Bottom Right: Three sailors on a tray. Japan, 1930's. $110.00-120.00.

Top: Two sailors on light blue plastic tray. 1930's. $60.00-65.00.

Clowns

Center: Three clowns attached — larger one is mustard. German, 1920. $120.00-160.00.

Bottom Left: Clowns dressed in red — these are made in Japan, 1930's. $95.00-110.00.

Bottom Right: Three clowns dressed in yellow and black. German, 1920-30. $120.00-160.00.

Monks

Top: Three comic monks on tray. Japan, 1960's. $40.00-50.00.

Left Center: Three monks attached. German, 1920-30. $120.00-140.00.

Right Center: Three monks on a tray, Carlton Ware. English, 1950's. $100.00-125.00.

Sports

Bottom: Boy with maroon shirt; balls are like soccer balls. German, 1930. $135.00-150.00.

Top Left: Carlton ware set — football. English, 1920-30. $120.00-160.00.

Top Right: Cricket player with three red balls. German, 1930-40. $130.00-150.00.

Center: Golfer — Crown Devon. English, 1930's. $135.00-155.00.

➤ Children

Bottom: Scottish children on tray. German made, 1920. $100.00-130.00.

Top Left: Two children with gramaphone. Japan, 1950. $95.00-110.00.

Top Right: Victorian child — mustard is the stump behind him. German, 1890's. $150.00-200.00.

Left Center: Kewpies. Possibly German, 1930's. $240.00-280.00.

Right Center: Two children praying with kitten. Japan, 1960. $95.00-110.00.

⭔ Miscellaneous People

Bottom: Old couple with fire in the fireplace. English, 1950's. $75.00-80.00.

Top Left: Three girls with tray of apples. German, 1920-30. $90.00-125.00.

Top Right: Bride, groom, and preacher on tray. Charming German set from the 1920's. $140.00-160.00.

Center: Three heads on tray. German, 1950's. $110.00-125.00.

Bottom Left: Beswick China. England, 1950's. $100.00-120.00.

Bottom Right: Gardener with two watering cans. Japan, 1950's. $60.00-90.00.

Top Left: Japanese set, 1950. $60.00-80.00.

Top Right: Two ladies, one standing, one sitting at a table set for tea. German, 1920-30. $95.00-130.00.

Center: English Carlton ware, three men in original box. 1940's. $150.00-200.00.

Bottom Left: Mr. Pickwick. German, 1930's. $120.00-160.00.

Bottom Right: German open salt and pepper, 1910. $90.00-120.00.

Top Left: Japanese set, 1950. This set and the one preceding are both of people in fancy dress. $80.00-90.00.

Top Right: Scotsman — one eye is pepper, the other is for mustard, and the mouth is the salt container; this is one of a series. German, 1920's. $160.00-200.00.

People: Black

Bottom Left: 1920's Jazz band. German. $300.00+.

Bottom Right: This head is part of the same series as the Scotsman. $250.00-350.00.

Top Left: Native type boys with hut. Japan, 1950. $70.00-90.00.

Top Right: Natives with drums for mustard. Japan, 1950. $80.00-100.00.

Bottom Left: These beautiful bisque heads were in my other book as just a pair of salt and pepper shakers — the tray and the mustard with lid, of course, makes the set much more valuable. German, 1920's. $200.00+.

Bottom Right: These black chefs are German — made in the 1930's. $100.00-150.00.

Top Left: These child chefs are also German — made in the 1930's. $135.00-165.00.

Top Right: Eastern blacks with urn. $90.00-100.00.

Center: African boys with beads and totem for mustard. $100.00-120.00.

Bottom: Another Japanese set — black boys with watermelon. $100.00-120.00.

Miscellaneous Sets

Top: Liquor bottle, cocktail shaker, and Seltzer bottle on tray 1960, plastic. $75.00-90.00.

Center: Tomatoes on a tray — these are among the most common. Tray is incised 4040 Germany. $40.00-50.00.

Bottom: Ducks and houses — these are the ½ timbered houses so popular in England. $65.00-75.00.

Top: Luster dogs; note spoon is tail. $95.00-110.00. Beautifully colored duck set by Noritake, Japan. $95.00-110.00.

Center: Indians, ceramic. Japan, 1960's. $95.00-110.00.

Bottom Left: Dwarf with two toadstools on tray — 1950 Crown Devon. English. $90.00-100.00.

Bottom Right: 1950's Indians, plastic. $65.00-70.00.

Luster Sets

Top: Two people in chairs on a boat. $95.00-110.00.

Center: Three-sail galleon, souvenir of State Capitol, Albany, New York Japan. $75.00-85.00.

Bottom Left: Fish set. Capitol Building, Havana, Cuba. There were many sets made with post card type scenes, sold as souvenirs. German. $65.00-85.00.

Bottom Right: Three cats on a tray — black tail is spoon. $95.00-110.00.

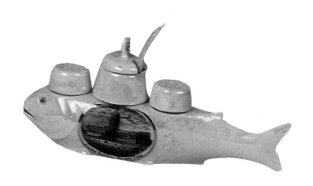

Top: Owls — small owl and large head are the shakers — the mustard is the larger owl's body. $65.00-75.00. Two dogs on a tray after a cat that sits atop the mustard. $75.00-90.00.

Center: Monkeys by Goebel. German. $120.00-150.00.

Bottom: A magnificent silver luster fish set; the top quarter of the head and the tip of the tail are the shakers. $125.00-145.00.

Top Left: Luster monkeys. German, 1920-30. $60.00-80.00.

Top Right: Lion is mustard; the cubs are the salt and pepper. German, 1920's. $120.00-140.00.

Center: Pink luster boat — another souvenir type; a miracle that all the delicate smokestacks were kept intact. $75.00-90.00.

Bottom: It is unusual and considered bad luck for an elephant's trunk to be pointed down. This set is German from the 1930's. $80.00-120.00.

Top: "Three Wise Monkeys from Margate" written on tray. German, 1930's. $50.00-80.00.

Center: This unusual elephant set was made in China in the 1960's. $75.00-90.00.

Bottom Left: This is a great Noah's Ark; it is German from the 1930's. $100.00-140.00.

Bottom Right: The camel is also German from the 1930's. $80.00-90.00.

Top Left: These dogs are Japanese; made in the 1960's. $75.00-90.00.

Top Right: Blue, white and gold luster swans. Japan, 1950's. $75.00-85.00.

Center: This set is Noritake like so many in my own collection, but I have never seen them with the tray and mustard before. Japan. $250.00-300.00.

Bottom Left: This wonderful little rabbit has ears for shakers and his head lifts off for the mustard. German, 1930's. $110.00-135.00.

Bottom Right: This is one of my favorite luster sets. German, 1920's. $200.00-225.00.

Top Left: Dutch type gold luster shoe. "A present from Herne Bay." German. $75.00-90.00.

Top Right: This is another set that I would love to have — the girl and boy are the shakers, and the chair is the mustard. Japan, 1920's. $160.00-180.00.

Center: Three clowns on tray; middle one splits in half for mustard. German, 1920's. $120.00-150.00.

Bottom: Woman and two children in boat; these are not as finely detailed as the German sets — or the Noritake Japanese sets. Japan, 1930's. $60.00-80.00.

Top: Gold and white luster airplane with red trim. French, 1960. $95.00-110.00.

Center: Two Indians in canoe. Japan, 1920's-30's. $60.00-80.00.

Bottom Left: Another of my "favorites," racing car. Made in Germany. $200.00+.

Bottom Right: This beautiful German clown is from the 1920's. $160.00-200.00.

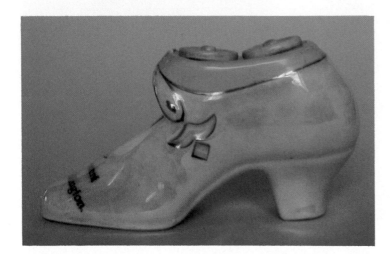

Top Left: Dutch woman with boy and girl attached. Japan, 1930. $95.00-110.00.

Top Right: Wonderful touring car. German, 1920-30. $140.00-165.00.

Center: Pearlized and gold luster shoe. German, 1930's. $95.00-110.00.

Bottom: Three galleons decorated with flowers. Japan, 1930's. $50.00-65.00.

Top Left: Zeppelin with scenic view. German, 1920-30. $100.00-125.00.

Top Right: Children with gramophone. Japan, 1930's. $95.00-110.00.

Center: Gold and white luster airplane viewed from above. French. $95.00-110.00.

Bottom: Yellow submarine. German, 1920-30. $130.00-150.00.

Food

Basket of fruit and vegetables salt and pepper shakers.

Top and Upper Center: All of these next sets are strange — Are they wearing bandannas, headbands, or do they have a toothache? $15.00-18.00.

Lower Center: Oversized cookies — there is a cookie jar to match. (Fattening!) $20.00-22.00.

Bottom Left: Beer and pretzels; the pretzels are by J. Rayton, California. $12.00-15.00. The beer mugs say 1933 — Happy Days. $8.00-10.00.

Bottom Right: Ice cream cones — not such an appetizing color. $8.00-10.00.

Top: Of all the fruit and vegetable people, these full figure variety are the most popular. Here are two sports sets: referees and baseball players. $50.00-55.00 per pair.

Upper Center: These vegetable head people are the same except for size. $40.00-45.00 per pair.

Lower Center: These shakers have a pearly glaze — the banana boat is different. $18.00-24.00.

Bottom: One-piece cucumbers and corn. $10.00-12.00. Vegetable head people. $25.00-35.00.

Top: Corn people. $20.00-30.00. Bananas. $20.00-30.00.

Upper Center: These vegetable heads come right off their bodies! Great gold trim. $30.00-35.00.

Lower Center: Bread people by Goebel. #73034 and 73035. $30.00-35.00. Latkes (potato pancakes) with fork and spoon arms are really different and delicious! $30.00-35.00.

Bottom: These little bisque head people are quite charming. $18.00-22.00.

Top: Two nice sets of fruit and vegetable people. $22.00-26.00.

Upper Center: Musical bananas. $35.00-45.00. Crazy coffee cups. $45.00-55.00.

Lower Center: Lots of musicians among the fruits and vegetables! $25.00-30.00.

Bottom: The pair on the left holding a tomato and garlic over their heads is one I've never seen before. $22.00-28.00. Watermelon heads. $22.00-28.00.

Holidays

Mother's Day

Top: Easter — ceramic eggs and a bunny with egg. $10.00-12.00.

Upper Center: Hallowe'en — witch and pumpkin — two versions. $25.00-30.00.

Lower Center: Thanksgiving — Hallmark. $15.00-18.00.

Bottom: Thanksgiving "Pilgrim's Progress," Fitz and Floyd. "Mayflower Mouse." $25.00-30.00.

Top: Valentines' Day — two hearts. $10.00-12.00. Lincoln's hat and axe. $10.00-12.00. Thanksgiving — Turkey and Girl dressed in orange. Napco. $12.00-18.00.

Center: Birthday cake and hearts and arrow. $20.00-25.00.

Bottom: Christmas — of course, the most popular in this category of any other holiday; the pair on the left by Fitz and Floyd. $25.00-35.00. The pair on the right by Omnibus. $15.00-20.00.

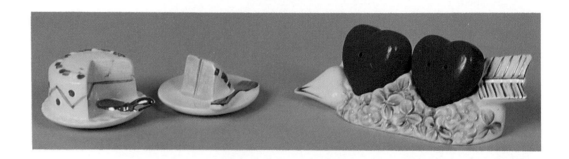

Top: Skating snowmen. $12.00-16.00. Goebel Santas — old mark — full Bee in V. $45.00-55.00.

Upper Center: New Year's Eve. Father time and clock. $20.00-25.00. Father time, the old year, and little boy, the new. $20.00-25.00.

Lower Center: Holt-Howard Santas probably from the 1950's. $25.00-30.00.

Bottom: Santa in sleigh and two reindeer. $22.00-30.00.

Top: These two striped sets are charming and a little different. $15.00-22.00 per pair.

Upper Center: Santas in space rockets. $22.00-26.00. Santas in houses. $12.00-16.00 per pair.

Lower Center: Cowboy (and girl) Santas. $22.00-25.00. Tennis-playing Santas. $15.00-18.00.

Bottom: Short and tall Santas. Tall ones are marked Mexico. $24.00-34.00 per pair.

Top: Choir children. $14.00-16.00 per pair.

Upper Center: Snowmen couple series. $14.00-16.00 per pair.

Lower Center: Set of caroling children. $14.00-18.00 per pair.

Bottom: Stylized Christmas trees and Santa children on bench. $16.00-18.00 per pair.

Top Left: These trees are marked Ukranian folk art. $15.00-18.00.

Top Right: Choir boys. $12.00-18.00.

Center: Jack-in-the-box snowman and tree and package. $15.00-20.00 per pair.

Bottom: Unusual Santa and reindeer. $18.00-22.00. Santa heads with "gingerbread" and very blue eyes. $18.00-22.00. Elephant Santas. $12.00-15.00.

Top: Santa and Dalmatian. Otagiri. $18.00-22.00. Wonderful snowman; cane is other shaker. $18.00-22.00.

Upper Center: Christmas ornament shakers — one-piece tree, and bow with bells and package mini. $8.00-10.00; $12.00-18.00; $18.00-22.00.

Lower Center: Two unusual sets...Santa on left looks like Holt Howard face, but girl he's with does not. Masquerade couple. $10.00-12.00; $18.00-20.00.

Bottom: Two more Christmas sets; I think a whole book could be done just on these. $12.00-14.00 per pair.

Wood Irons, a chrome boat from England, and a Ball jar shaker.

Top: Silver color pigs, and horse heads. $15.00-18.00.

Upper Center: Two bicycles – one in silver tone, one in brass. $20.00-25.00.

Lower Center: Four donkey carriers — four sizes, in silver and copper color. $10.00-12.00.

Bottom: Cloisonne type birds — these are a combination of metal and pottery; the colored areas are separated by thin metal bands; these are very beautiful. $30.00-40.00.

Top: Two pairs of squirrels. $12.00-15.00.

Center: These two sets are sterling silver and very nicely detailed. The golfers, and the standing couple — per pair. $95.00-125.00.

Bottom Left: These Oriental lanterns are stamped Occupied Japan. $18.00-24.00.

Bottom Right: Penguins — these are really sleek. $24.00-28.00. Porpoises standing on a wave. $12.00-14.00.

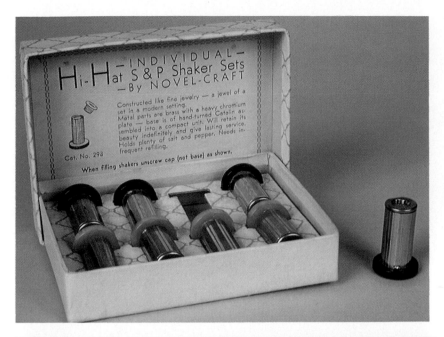

Top: Art Deco chrome shakers in the original box — bakelite trim. $45.00-65.00 set.

Upper Center: Prayers and shakers all in one metal base. $8.00-10.00. Owl with plastic shakers and box for saccharin. $8.00-10.00.

Lower Center: Amish people — pot metal painted. $8.00-10.00.

Bottom: Pennsylvania Dutch painted footballs and scoops. $8.00-10.00.

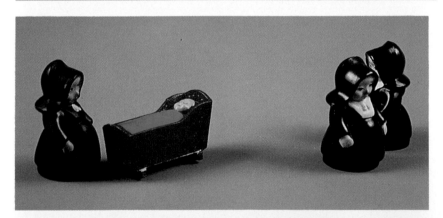

Top Left: Policeman and "Lady of the Night." There's also a set like this with a policeman and a thug — how to really grace your dinner table. $35.00-40.00.

Top Right: Spool people — the heads are just a cover for the shakers. $15.00-18.00.

Upper Center: I saw these advertised in the New York Times, and enjoyed the pun on Shaker tables. They were made by Claude Graham 3d, a woodworker in Jacksonville, Fla., using the design of the Shakers who settled in the United States in 1774. They are known for the simplicity and beauty of their designs. $28.00 per pair.

Lower Center: Carved shakers from Africa. $8.00-10.00.

Bottom: These are not actually wood, but carved from pits or nuts. $10.00-15.00.

Top: The wooden rabbits are nicely painted. $8.00-10.00.

Center: The wooden ducks have tails that unscrew to fill them. $10.00-14.00. Bookcase — perfect for doll house furniture. $10.00-12.00.

Bottom Left: More furniture — radio and clock. $10.00-14.00.

Bottom Right: Two sets of wooden snowmen — large and small. $12.00-14.00.

Top: These three sets are from Poland, and are decorated as folk art. $12.00-14.00.

Upper Center: The pair on the left, the boy with two pots, is from Yugoslavia — his face is charming. $18.00-22.00. The boy on the right, holding two tomatoes, is from Japan. $15.00-18.00.

Lower Center: The couple on the right are marked USSR; the other set is Japanese. $12.00-15.00.

Bottom: The dogs are unusual in that the part that screws on is all glass. The lamps are a replica of miniature oil lamps. $15.00-18.00.

Top: These two sets are Japanese. $10.00-12.00.

Upper Center: Two sets marked USSR — these should really become collector's items. $12.00-15.00.

Lower Center: These are Czechoslovakian glass with china heads. They come in different forms and colors. $30.00-35.00.

Bottom Left: These have to be the epitome of tacky — glass, stones and plastic tops; I wonder if a collection of 20 or more would make them beautiful! (or 20 times as ugly?) $6.00-8.00.

Bottom Right: Combination wood and rope. $6.00-8.00.

Top: Perhaps these will convince collectors that there is variety in wood sets. $8.00-10.00.

Upper Center: These camels are a combination of glass, metal and wood. $15.00-20.00.

Lower Center: Exquisitely carved and detailed shoes. $40.00-50.00.

Bottom: These glass sets look hand blown; the top hat is a salt dish with spoon, and the pepper is the cane. $25.00-30.00. Black and white striped penguins. $25.00-30.00. Blown glass bottles. $25.00-30.00.

Top: These glass animals were probably candy containers — after the candy was gone, they served a dual purpose and became shakers. $20.00-22.00.

Upper Center: Glass paint tubes with screw on caps. $18.00-20.00.

Lower Center: Glass fruit — these have an inverted funnel inside. $22.00-26.00.

Bottom: More beautiful blown glass shakers — these are swans. $24.00-28.00.

People

Around the World

Top: This Mexican couple has much nicer detail than most. $18.00-20.00. Cactus. $15.00-18.00.

Center: Mexicans — these are Elbee Art. $16.00-18.00.

Bottom: Two Mexican couples — the couple on the right are fighting and she is holding a knife behind her back. Pair on left, $15.00-18.00; pair on right, $30.00-35.00.

Top: Two more Mexican sets — cactus and anything western are very collectible right now. $12.00-15.00.

Upper Center: I love the set with the flower pot — the cactus lifts out and is the other shaker. . .each set. $15.00-18.00.

Lower Center: Two sets of Mexican clay pottery — ducks and people. $8.00-10.00.

Bottom: Stylized Mexicans dispense the salt and pepper through eye and nose; the other couple are brightly painted, and she carries a tray of fruit on her head. Good for posture! $12.00-15.00.

Top: The Oriental farmer is carrying two baskets with pig's heads. $24.00-28.00. An unusual old Oriental couple. $15.00-18.00.

Upper Center: Mexican on his burro, and on tray with cactus. $10.00-12.00.

Lower Center: Eskimo couple. $10.00-12.00. Oriental couple. $8.00-10.00.

Bottom: Two pairs of rather unusual Oriental people. $15.00-18.00.

Top: Plastic ivory-colored screaming couple. $10.00-12.00. Chinese dragons. $20.00-24.00.

Center: Two lovely Oriental sets — the girl with urn of fruit. $20.00-22.00. The tall woman holding tomatoes. $26.00-30.00.

Bottom: Eastern pair, seated — Occupied Japan. $20.00-22.00. Windmills also Occupied Japan. $18.00-22.00.

Top: Two Danish girls, and a couple with silver luster decorations. Danish girls, $24.00-28.00; couple, $40.00-50.00.

Upper Center: Two Hawaiian sets. $14.00-18.00.

The following sets belong to a series; they are marked "Josep Originals — Japan" and are approximately 4" tall. There is a paper label with the country name. $18.00-24.00 per pair.

Lower Center: England and France.

Bottom: Italy and Russia.

Top: Mexico and Spain.

Upper Center: China and Switzerland.

Lower Center: Holland and Germany.

Bottom: Ireland and Scotland.

This is another series of people from different countries. Mother and child sets Napco 1960 stamped and 3N4970 on bottom on each set; the mothers are 3¼" tall. $18.00-24.00 per pair.

Top: Japanese and perhaps Siamese.

Center: United States and Holland.

Bottom: Two charming Irish couples. $12.00-14.00.

Top: Cowboy couple and boot and saddle. $12.00-15.00.

Center: Cowboy and cactus by Arcadia ceramics, California. $35.00-45.00.

Bottom: Cowboys — made in Czechoslovakia. $12.00-15.00. Anthropomorphic cacti. $26.00-28.00.

Top: These two cowboys are very similar, but the set with the white hat is ceramic, the one with the black hat is metal (hat comes off and is one shaker; the head is the other). $18.00-24.00.

Upper Center: Guns in holsters, one-piece cactus and cowboy gloves. $16.00-18.00 per pair.

Lower Center: Nice pair of ceramic horses. $10.00-12.00. This cowboy looks young to be so ferocious. $18.00-24.00.

Bottom: Leather Indian drums with real feathers. $8.00-10.00. Boot and saddle. $10.00-12.00.

Top: More anthropomorphic cacti — the pair on the left is a couple. $26.00-32.00. Cactus heads. $26.00-32.00.

Upper Center: Cowboy and Indian, each carrying shakers. $20.00-22.00 per pair.

Lower Center: Indians in canoe; mother Indian and papoose. $14.00-18.00 per pair.

Bottom Left: Indians on horseback. $20.00-22.00 per pair.

Bottom Right: Two more Indians on rearing horses. $16.00-18.00 per pair.

Top: Indian children with faces that look anything but Native American! $14.00-18.00.

Center: Four-piece set — Thrifco Ceramics Japan. $30.00-40.00.

Bottom: Nice condiment set in luster. $45.00-50.00. Native American and his squaw; tepee is mustard. $25.00-35.00.

People: General

Top: This is a classic set, the football player holding the other player's head. The one on the ground without a head is holding the ball for the kicker. $50.00-60.00. Baseball players. $50.00-60.00.

Center: Baseball players — these are very popular and they appeal to sports collectors as well as salt and pepper collectors. $50.00-60.00. Boxers. $35.00-40.00.

Bottom: Baseball players and referees — two great sets — these are heavy and have some age; probably from the 1940's or 1950's. $50.00-60.00.

Top: These are cartoon sports players marked Napco, 1958. $14.00-16.00.

Center: Deep sea diver and fish — a nice set — good color and glaze. Fisherman diving to catch his fish; the one that almost got away! $30.00-35.00.

Bottom Left: The tall and the short of it: two pairs of skiers. $20.00-24.00.

Bottom Right: The surfer on his surfboard is one pair. $28.00-32.00. Scallop shells. $12.00-14.00.

Top Left: A set of four toy soldiers. $20.00-22.00 set.

Top Right: Clowns are very popular and there are hundreds of clown sets. The pair on the left look like Emmet Kelley. $50.00-60.00. Clown on clown. $16.00-18.00.

Center: These clowns are identical except for the color of their hats and buttons. $15.00-18.00.

Bottom: These clowns are by Napco and marked 1957. $22.00-24.00.

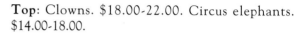

Top: Clowns. $18.00-22.00. Circus elephants. $14.00-18.00.

Upper Center: Precarious poses for the dinner table, but all right for the circus. $16.00-18.00.

Lower Center: These two sets are chalkware, and the paint is in amazingly good condition. $14.00-18.00.

Bottom: Elbee Art sailor in his boat. $22.00-24.00. St. Lawrence Seaway ship. $22.00-24.00.

Top: Two small couples playing instruments. $18.00-20.00.

Upper Center: The two little girls on the left are very stylized. $18.00-22.00. The children on the right are reminiscent of the 1940's. $35.00-40.00.

Lower Center: Babies playing at fishing, shooting, baseball, and boxing. $15.00-18.00 per pair.

Bottom: Charming sailors. $24.00-28.00. Ocean liner. $18.00-22.00.

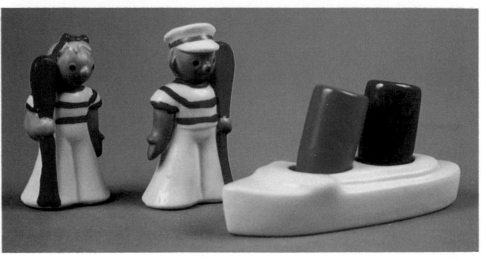

Top Left and Top Right: The salt and pepper shakers are Stanley and Livingstone, explorers in Africa. Dr. Livingstone was buried with high honors in Westminster Abbey after being felled by dysentery. $50.00-60.00.

Center: Two Victorian type sets; very delicate. $20.00-24.00.

Bottom: Two pairs of girls dressed in hearts. $16.00-18.00.

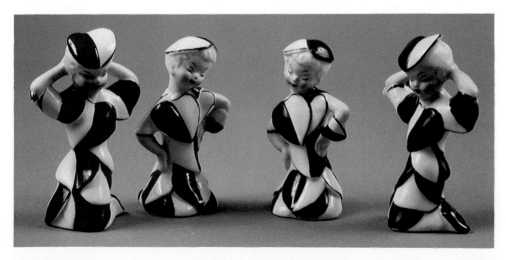

Top: The Art Deco lady heads are magnificent. $125.00-150.00. Bellhop with two eggs on tray — great sets! $125.00-150.00.

Center: Fancy dress couple. $14.00-16.00. Man in the moon. $24.00-26.00.

Bottom: Six friars; they can be paired according to what they're doing. $16.00-18.00.

Top: Comic pair. $15.00-18.00.

Center: Boy and girl with umbrellas — Napco, 1956. $12.00-16.00. Pixie chefs marked with #1C2426; they have rubber stoppers. $18.00-20.00.

Bottom: The band leader and his podium are a separate set — three other pairs. $40.00-45.00 set.

Top: A pair of Nuns. $15.00-18.00.

Center and Bottom: These tiny chefs were made in Germany. There is a man and a woman to each set. $20.00-25.00 per pair.

Top: The nude in the bathtub, and the nude in the keyhole are much less common than the third set. Keyhole. $45.00-55.00. Bathtub. $40.00-45.00. Headless nude. $12.00-15.00.

Center: Heads made of some type of Japanese lacquer. $10.00-12.00. Small heads. $10.00-12.00.

Bottom Right and Bottom Left: Set on the left fit together like a puzzle. $60.00-70.00. Turnabout couple. $45.00-50.00.

Top: Alcatraz heads — note beard. $22.00-26.00.

Center and Bottom Left: Toby mug type heads. $8.00-10.00.

Bottom Right: These two sets look like an ad for a razor company. $14.00-16.00 per pair.

Top: Two Davy Crockett type boys in canoe. $18.00-20.00. Boy and pelican (?). $8.00-10.00.

Center: Most of these children in this style of large hat are in orange; this set is unusual in its coloration. $10.00-12.00. Hugging children with drop pyjamas. $10.00-12.00.

Bottom Left: Drunk and lamppost set. $12.00-14.00.

Bottom Right: Drunk and lamppost, and drunk on park bench. $14.00-16.00 per pair.

Top: Toy soldiers and hugging couple. $18.00-22.00 per pair.

Center: This Amish woman in her rocker is ceramic; most are metal. $12.00-14.00.

Bottom Left: The kissing couple have a lovely glaze and nice features. $12.00-16.00. Baby in cradle — Omnibus — made in Korea. $8.00-10.00.

Bottom Right: There are several different versions of these green monsters. $35.00-45.00.

Top: Dr. and dog nurse on bench. $12.00-15.00. Two little girls with pigtails. $8.00-10.00.

Upper Center: Space creatures. $10.00-15.00. Astronaut and rocket. $26.00-28.00.

Lower Center: Two German sets — nice glazes and colors. $26.00-30.00 per pair.

Bottom: Babies born in the cabbage patch. $14.00-16.00. Children are German made. $28.00-30.00.

Top Left: Another German set —
they look mad! $24.00-28.00.

Top Right: Ma and Old Doc shakers
by Imperial Porcelain. These Blue
Ridge Mountain and American folk-
lore figures were created by cartoon-
ist Paul Webb. The Imperial
Porcelain Co. was founded in
Zanesville, Ohio in 1947. They
closed in 1960. $95.00-110.00.

Center: These little bellhops and
maid are really charming —
German. $35.00-45.00 per pair.

Bottom: The girls with the Dutch
hats are Japanese luster. $35.00-
45.00. The fisherman set is German.
$40.00-45.00.

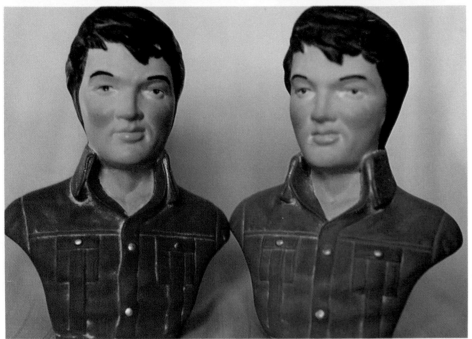

Top Right: Two sets of Elvis that are not figural. I purchased these in the gift shop at "Graceland." $35.00-45.00.

Top Left: Dean Martin and Jerry Lewis — unmarked. $300.00+.

Center: Bill Fisher had these busts of Elvis made in a Ceramic Shop in Ohio. Bill and Joyce were in charge of the Ohio Convention in 1989 and had a mold reduced down to shakers size. He had 200 of them made and they cost $35.00 a pair in 1989. Since there were never more than the original 200 made, I would estimate the price to be at least tripled. (They were made in two color combinations.) $150.00-200.00.

━━━━━ People: Black

Bottom: Two Mammies — one with a happy face, the other frowning, 3". $45.00-50.00. Bald man with a slice of watermelon. $35.00-45.00.

Top Left: A very rare advertising set from the Royal Hotel in Boise, Idaho. These were made in Japan; only a few sets were made and they were never used. 4¼". $195.00-225.00.

Top Right: Boy and girl. 2½". $50.00-65.00. This three-piece set with the man carrying a yoke with two baskets has a female counterpart. 5". $75.00-85.00.

Center: Boy sitting on a cotton bale — sticker reads Iowa State Fair, 1955. 3½". $65.00-85.00. Three-piece set — chef with big feet; salt and pepper containers are milk cans. $95.00-110.00.

Bottom: Wooden set — not the more common Liza and Rastus. Souvenir from the Ozarks. $20.00-30.00. These heads are wood and the bottoms are metal bells. Japan, 4". $40.00-45.00.

Top Left: Elderly couple — he has beard and cane; she carries a shopping basket. 3", made in Japan. Scarce. $125.00-140.00. This boy with watermelon is different from the usually seen one as he has crossed legs. A planter was made in the same design and color. Japan, 4¼". Hard to find. $95.00-110.00.

Top Right: The graduates: sitting on tree stumps. He holds a diploma and flower; she holds a book. $55.00-65.00.

Upper Center: Winking chef and cook babies — similar to the pat-a-cake twins, but these are wearing chef's hats. $100.00-125.00. Wonderful boy/girl set with moveable eyes. She serves a cake; he serves a pie. Enesco Imports, Japan. $125.00-145.00.

Lower Center: Luzianne coffee; the pair on the left are ceramic — these matched a cookie jar marked USA. 4¼". $175.00-180.00. Pair on right are plastic marked "F&F Die Works" 5¼". $125.00-130.00.

Bottom: Coon Chicken Inn restaurant souvenir shakers. Gold letters on back of man at left say "Coon Chicken Inn." Same is scratched on back of man in pair on right. No mark; very sought after. $375.00-400.00.

Top: Three-piece flat back Mammy set, marked "Carlah Studios, Carl Roger Ceramics, Laguna Beach, Calif," 5½" tall. $250.00-275.00 (3 pc.).

Center: These are two different sets of the Mammy and Butler. The pair on the left are 5" tall and the pair on the right are 4¾". Both sets are marked Japan. $125.00-130.00, $90.00-95.00.

Bottom Left and Right: Before and After — turnabout couple. $150.00-175.00.

Top: Men with guitar and drum — bisque. $30.00-35.00. Chefs serving drinks — cold paint. $75.00-85.00.

Upper Center: Man and woman sitting on a stump; these are very unusual. Marked "1950 Deebs Col's Ohio." 5" tall. Porgy & Bess? $85.00-95.00. Couple in fancy clothes; woman showing off her bare feet. $100.00-125.00.

Lower Center: Mammy with chef heads — 3½" tall, marked 7859. $80.00-90.00. Mammy teapot heads. These have matching cookie jar and teapot. $120.00-125.00.

Bottom: This is a different version of the more common heads. $40.00-45.00. Cold painted head and shoulders. 3", marked Made in Japan. $40.00-45.00.

Top: Baby in basket with bottle. $55.00-60.00.

Upper Center: Mammy and chef heads — Mammy sticking out tongue, and chef winking. $85.00-100.00. Mammy and chef — paint under glaze. $60.00-65.00.

Lower Center: Both of these sets have the same motif but are painted completely differently. Both sets are made in Japan; the set on the right says Windsor on one dish and Canada on the other. $85.00-100.00.

Bottom: These sets all have variations in color and design. $80.00-95.00. Similar set in cold paint; has matching cookie jar. $50.00-55.00.

Top: These shakers were made by Brayton Laguna Pottery founded in Southern California in 1927. They were made in several colors and had matching cookie jars. These are 5½" tall. $95.00-110.00.

Upper Center: The pair on the left are similar to the common red, white and blue Mammy and chef sets, but these have oversize heads. Paper label says "Empress Made in Japan." $55.00-60.00. This is an unusual set. Mammy is showing her petticoat and the chef is sticking out his tongue. 5½" tall. $70.00-75.00.

Lower Center: Two sets with pink clothes. Set on right has decal showing the U.S. Capitol and says "Washington, D.C." $55.00-65.00 per pair.

Bottom: Two versions of blinking eye shakers. Right pair has sticker that says "Souvenir of Indian Lake, Ohio." $45.00-50.00.

Top: Two versions of the 8½" range shakers. The Mammy on the left has a tilted head and tulips on her apron. $110.00-115.00. The unusual thing about the set on the right is the S and P painted on the spoons. Both of these have the red cold painted. Paper label says "Made in Japan — Thames — hand painted. $110.00-115.00.

Center: The Mammy on the left has gray hair, 6½" tall. $85.00-90.00. The pair on the right are an unusual pastel color and are 7½". $85.00-90.00.

Bottom: All black set with gold trim. $30.00-35.00. Children reading books in rocking chairs. Their eyes blink as the rocker moves, and the holes are in the back of the chairs. $55.00-65.00.

Top: Left: 2½" cannibal looking up at white man in pot. Japan. $95.00-110.00. Right: Very unusual black man and woman huggers, 3". $85.00-95.00.

Upper Center: Two sets of farmers — paper label says "Enesco Imports, Japan." $75.00-80.00.

Lower Center: White sea captain with black ship's mate. $55.00-60.00. 5" chefs marked K2218 A Napco Ceramic. $30.00-35.00.

Bottom: These are "Naughties." Pair on left are two naked children in sleeping position. Turn them over, and they say "Hi, Nosey" imprinted in the ceramic. 1½" high by 3½" long. $55.00-65.00. The pair on the right is quite common in the white version. $45.00-55.00.

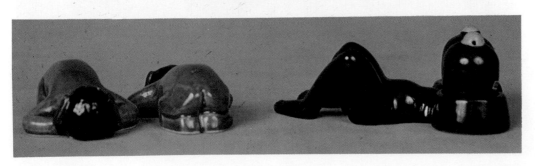

Top: Boy sitting with whole watermelon; girl sitting with legs outstretched and watermelon slice on her legs. $50.00-65.00 per pair.

Upper Center: These two sets are older versions of other similar sets that have previously been pictured. They have greater detail than the other sets. Both are Japanese made. $85.00-90.00, 70.00-75.00.

Lower Center: Three different versions of black boy on elephant. In the set on the left the salt pours out of top of elephant's head; 6" tall, marked "made in Japan." $65.00-70.00. Center set: salt pours out of the eyes and mouth — marked Ceramic Arts Studio, Madison, Wisc. $95.00-110.00. Pair on the right: Salt pours out of the eyes only. Marked Japan Importing Company, New York City, N.Y. $95.00-100.00.

Bottom: Solid pink set also comes in other colors. Marked "877 USA" impressed in the ceramic. $45.00-50.00. Black glazed set of two girls trimmed in gold with cloth aprons. Lift cloth and it says S and P in gold. $60.00-65.00.

Top: Bellhop with suitcase, 2¾". $55.00-70.00. One-piece bellhop. $85.00-100.00.

Upper Center: Two chalkware sets. Left: 2" heads with holes in the eyes. Blue ink stamp on bottom says USA. $70.00-75.00. Right: Bride and groom. $50.00-55.00.

Lower Center: Three versions of chalkware Mammies sitting with their legs crossed. $30.00-35.00; $40.00-45.00; $30.00-35.00.

Bottom: Busts of Joe Louis and a white boxer (?) nice quality. $45.00-50.00. 4" tall crude Mammies — may have had cold paint at one time. $25.00-30.00.

Top: Three-piece wooden porters. They were made in Japan, and the larger one is 7½"; the smaller 4¾". $30.00-35.00 each.

Center: The Mammy with two buckets comes in many colors and has a matching chef. Made in Japan. $85.00-100.00. The bellhop with eggs on tray is a beautiful Art Deco set that I would love to have in my own collection — bellhops definitely speak of a time gone by and are very nostalgic in design and image. $150.00-175.00.

Bottom: Man and woman standing on a tray with tree as handle. Unusual. $100.00-115.00. There is a matching girl in this set which has already appeared in my first book on page 64. $95.00-110.00.

Top: It was hard to decide whether to put this set in the chapter on condiments or in this chapter on blacks. This set is all one piece — the two smaller heads are the shakers. These are marked "36 Germany." $150.00-200.00.

Upper Center: Two sets of oil, vinegar, salt and pepper. The set on the left is 5" tall, of cold paint, and marked Japan. $95.00-100.00. The set on the right has also appeared in my first book, but this set has far more interesting coloring and clothing (the hands have corks attached and remove for pouring). $135.00-140.00.

Lower Center: Another oil and vinegar set — this one the heads are removable. Mammy pushing cart is unusual. Both sets have paper label "Enesco Imports Japan." $130.00-135.00, 140.00-145.00.

Bottom: Two sets of shakers: range size and table size with matching grease jar. $150.00-175.00. 5" shakers with log cabin grease jar. $130.00-135.00.

Top: 5¼" chef holding pitcher is attached to the stand. Marked "Fairyland China, Japan." There are other versions of this set; one with a Mammy holding an orange, and a smaller one with a young bellhop. $90.00-110.00.

Upper Center: 5" range shakers with white man in pot. The smaller shakers were probably for the table. $150.00-175.00.

Lower Center: Odd shaped men in turbans; pair on left German, pair on right Bavarian. $60.00-65.00.

Bottom: Black boys with melon slices — Japan. $65.00-85.00. Egg-shaped hand painted man and woman, marked Beasil. $25.00-30.00.

Top: Mother and baby, and native boy with watermelon. $30.00-40.00 per set.

Upper Center: Native head with bone — the bone is one shaker. $90.00-95.00. Native with grass hut marked Japan. $35.00-45.00.

Lower Center: Flirting boy and girl and boy with palm tree. $25.00-30.00 per set.

Bottom: These are very crude and hardly painted. $20.00-25.00. Native boy with alligator. $45.00-50.00.

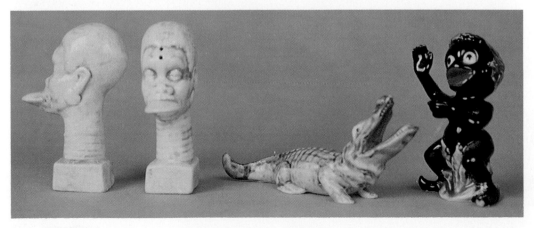

Top: These two sets are part of a series. The pair on the left are 5½" tall and the boy on the right has a backpack; The other pair shows one boy reading a book. They have an iridescent glaze. $30.00-35.00 per pair.

Center: Boy holding two trays filled with berries. $95.00-125.00. Red cap porter with two suitcases. $95.00-125.00. Shoe shine boy with shoe stand. $95.00-125.00.

Bottom: Three sets of chalkware — these are relatively new. $20.00-30.00 per pair.

Top: New set of four musicians — nicely crafted. $35.00-50.00 (four).

Center: Three chefs — the middle one is just a figurine. $45.00-55.00.

Bottom: African type condiment set — the full figures are the shakers. The head lifts off the middle to reveal the mustard pot; the tongue is the spoon. $150.00-175.00.

Top: Two more sets of chalkware — the set on the left is new; the set on the right is old — I have seen it in many colors. $25.00-30.00, $40.00-45.00.

Center: Native boy on elephant. He is the lid for the mustard; the shakers are the two baskets hanging on the sides. $100.00-125.00. Boy on hippo. This is most unusual, and at first I doubted that it was a pair. It is more common to find the boy on an alligator. However, the bottom of the boy has an indented triangle that fits on a raised triangle on the back of the hippo. $135.00-150.00.

Bottom: Native boy with alligator. $50.00-75.00.

Top: Natives on drums. The drum is a shaker as well as the figure. $80.00-100.00 per pair.

Center: Chefs — one with bottle and mug; the other with tray. $200.00-250.00.

Bottom Left: Mammy and chef heads on spoon rests. $200.00-250.00.

Bottom Right: Native lady with gold earrings — head is one shaker; the neck is the other. $100.00-125.00.

Nodders

There are three different sets of elephant nodders pictured here. Note that the clowns' hat and suit are different in all three as are the blankets on the elephants. $250.00-300.00.

There are four pairs of walking pigs. Again, the clothes and colors are different. $200.00-250.00.

Top: Snake charmer and snake in basket. $200.00-225.00.

Center: Birds in log with mustard pot on end. $75.00-125.00.

Bottom Left: Bride and Groom Pigs; rare. $125.00-150.00.

Bottom Right: These sailboat nodders are nice since they repeated the sailboat theme on the base; many have the common white base with roses no matter what the shakers are. $60.00-75.00.

Top Left: Full figured Indians — again in a related base. $60.00-75.00.

Top Right: Two people: one with a sad face, and one happy. $125.00-200.00.

Center: This couple does appear in Melva Davern's second book but again the colors are different. The boy is carrying a butterfly net. $250.00-300.00.

Bottom: Camel with nodding monkeys. The blanket on this camel is the same as that on one of the elephants. The camel nodder in my first book has a different blanket than this, but the same as on one of these elephants. I would presume therefore, that the camel and elephant nodders were made by the same company. $250.00-300.00.

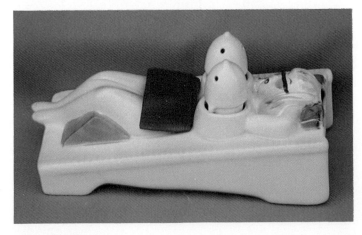

Top Left: This boy reading a book is wonderful; his head nods. The book is the other shaker, but doesn't nod. $150.00-200.00.

Top Right: Fish nodder. $85.00-95.00.

Center: This deer nodder is almost twice the size of the common set. $35.00-40.00.

Bottom: Nude nodder; this is a new set — towel is the mustard cover. Reissue of 1980 set by Five and Dime, Inc. $30.00.

Top: These teddy bears are larger than those usually seen. $30.00-35.00. This black woman is different from the others I have seen. The body head is poorly defined, and the whole set is crudely made. Head nods up and down. $100.00-110.00.

Upper Center: Canaries in common base. $25.00-30.00. Birds in a log base feeding their babies. When they "nod" they almost look like they're feeding their young. $35.00-45.00.

Lower Center: These flamingos are different because they're covered with shells. $40.00-45.00.

Bottom: These two sets of chick nodders look almost identical, but the set on the left is ceramic, and the set on the right is plastic. The ceramic set is marked "Made in China" in red. The yellow chick rocks from side to side, and the black and white one rocks up and down. $40.00-50.00. The plastic set also nods sideways and up and down. $35.00-40.00.

Top: This nodder is my very favorite. My husband found it in London, at Bermondsey's Market. The head nods, and the hand on the right, holding the gun also nods. $250.00-300.00.

Center: Two donkeys in a condiment base; I have seen this same base with race horses. $75.00-95.00. Monkey and baby — each nods in different direction. $75.00-95.00.

Bottom: More birds in a log type base. $45.00-55.00 per set. Chickens in a nest with mustard; the knob of the mustard lid is a baby chick. $45.00-55.00.

Places

BONNEVILLE | DAM OREGON

MT. HOOD | OREGON

I call these "split scenes" for want of a better name. These photographs were taken by David Peters of Venice, California, and the six sets following belong to him and his wife, Jan. I would be curious to know if anyone has seen others in this series.

Top: Bonneville Dam, Oregon. $18.00-22.00.

Center: Mt. Hood, Oregon. $18.00-22.00.

Bottom: White Sands, New Mexico and Grand Canyon National Park. $18.00-22.00 per pair.

WHITE SANDS | NEW MEXICO | GRAND CANYON | NAT'L PARK

Top: This set is of Yellowstone Park also marked Old Faithful. One other pair that I know of was in my third book; it is of Aquarena, San Marcos, Texas (p. 58).

Center: Sandia Crest, New Mexico, The Grotto of the Blessed Virgin Mary, and Mt. Rainier, Washington. $18.00-22.00 per pair.

Bottom: These are curious, as they are not of a geographical place, but certainly made and marked the same way. $18.00-22.00.

Top: This is an interesting set — the shakers are the towers in the gate. The material is a bisque-like ceramic. $20.00-30.00.

Center: This is a very rare set from 1939 New York World's Fair in its original box. It is from the collection of Walter Rhodes, Connecticut; he was kind enough to bring it to Hot Shots in Stratford, while we were doing a shoot. The set has "158 Bright" printed under the box; also says copyright NY World's Fair. $110.00-135.00.

Bottom: An unusual pair from the 1962 Seattle World's Fair. $35.00-50.00.

Top: The hats are from the Loretta Lynn Dude Ranch, Dixon, Tennessee. $15.00-20.00. The clowns are from Las Vegas, and the axe and log are from Springfield, Illinois, home of Lincoln. (Marked Lincoln's tomb.) $12.00-18.00 per pair.

Center: The S.S. Lurline — George Wallace's boat: Lurline was his wife's name. $12.00-18.00. The mugs say "I survived the earthquake at Universal Studios." $18.00-22.00.

Bottom: The pair on the left are from Salt Lake City — The Mormon Temple. $15.00-18.00. The ground hogs are from Punxsutawney, Pennsylvania; the place where the ground hog comes out to see his shadow and predict how many more weeks of winter there will be. $15.00-18.00.

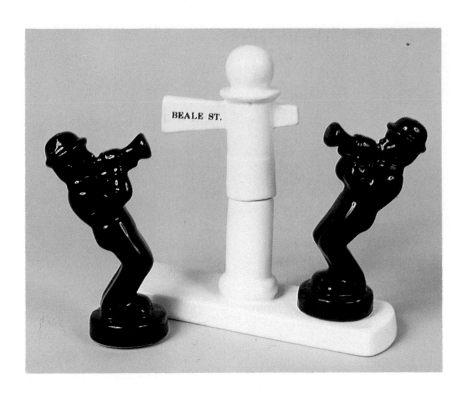

Top: Jazz Musicians on stand that says Beale Street, from Memphis. $12.00-15.00.

Center: Three pairs of metal sets: The two outside sets say "The World's only corn palace, Mitchell, South Dakota." $35.00-45.00. The center set is a pair of cars on a tray from the Grand Canyon. $18.00-22.00.

Bottom: Brown Derby hats — heavy pottery says "Hollywood, Calif." in mold on bottom of hats. $20.00-35.00. Another set of Mormon Tabernacle and Temple. Lightweight. $10.00-12.00.

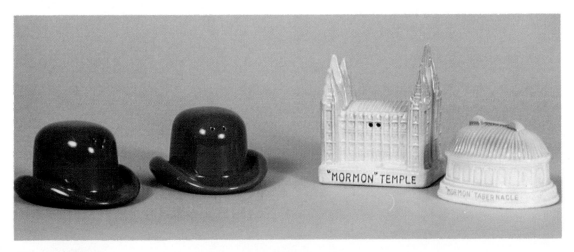

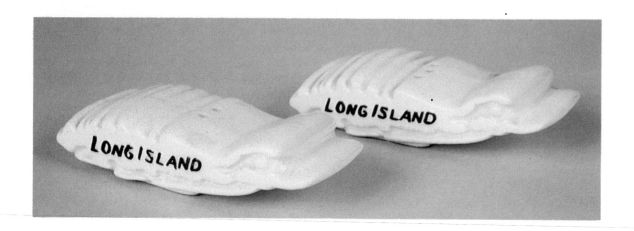

Top: These are part of the Milford Pottery State series. $18.00-25.00.

Center: These sets look tacky alone — but in series, they have a certain charm, or are they just three times as "tacky?" $6.00-8.00 per pair.

Bottom: I also find these sets more interesting in a series. They show various points of interest in each state; it would be a challenge to find all 50 of them (if they exist). $6.00-8.00. per pair.

Plastic

Plastic umbrellas on stand from the 1950's.

Top: This is the mystery set of the decade. I've been trying to find out something about it through the S&P Newsletter, and by asking experienced collectors. No one seems to know who "Salty Kennedy" and "Peppy Cohen" are. Help! $10.00-15.00.

Center: Snow domes are becoming highly collectible in their own right; ones that are also salt and pepper shakers are even more desirable as they appeal to two different categories of collectors. Tall domes — Florida; TV type shaker "The Ozarks." $20.00-35.00 each. Canadian Eskimo. $20.00-35.00.

Bottom: The pair on the left are called Aquabatics. They consist of a black and a white ball with a clear ring all around. Within the ring are brightly colored plastic fruit. 1989 made in England. $20.00-25.00. Glitter egg by Applause...New for Easter of 1991. Colors as shown purple and yellow, or pink and turquoise. Top of egg screws off for salt and pepper; bottom is like a snow dome filled with water and glitter. $8.00-10.00.

Top: These two sets of children are on a puzzle type base that fits together. $25.00-30.00 per pair.

Upper Center: Eskimos. $25.00-35.00. Royal Canadian Mounted Police and Indian — plaque says Canada. $25.00-35.00.

Lower Center: There are dozens of sets of mice and cheese, but this is the first set I've seen in plastic. The two sets are the same except for color. $15.00-20.00.

Bottom: These sets are Bakelite — early plastic — the birds are the most unusual and have wire legs. $40.00-55.00 per pair.

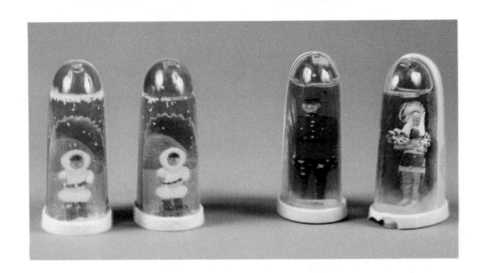

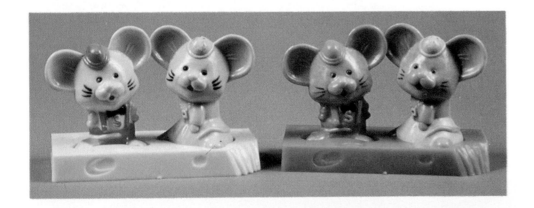

Top: Scotsman with two eggs, and Elf with two eggs. The set on the right says "H,B, Outpost, Southampton, Canada. $12.00-18.00 per set.

Upper Center: Gum ball machines and collage of beans. $15.00-20.00 per set.

Lower Center: Roly Polys; again, these are unusual in plastic. $15.00-20.00. Happy and sad eggs in shoes. $10.00-15.00.

Bottom: Another Bakelite group — mushrooms and a condiment set. $40.00-55.00 per pair.

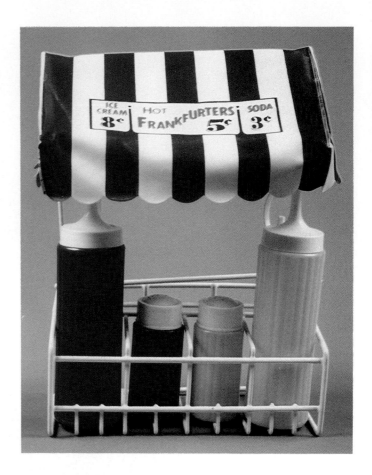

Top Left: This radio is marked ICP. It is unusual to have a radio designed for the kitchen that holds condiments. $45.00-50.00.

Top Right: This set is not old, but very colorful. $10.00-12.00.

Bottom: This set of canaries on branch is a proto-type for an advertising company; you could order the set with your own message and logo. $15.00-20.00. Rockets with flamingos — an unlikely combination. $8.00-10.00.

Top: Walking salt and pepper in box. Please pass the salt! Cooks' tools, 1984; H&P Mayer Company. $15.00-20.00.

Upper Center: Tiny couple with large eggs. $12.00-15.00. I bought this set of pool balls at Barney's, New York. It is a very heavy shiny plastic, and was made in France. $35.00-40.00.

Bottom Left: These fish stand on the hooks of the anchor; the salt and pepper come out of the plastic "stoppers" in their mouths. $25.00-35.00.

Bottom Right: These are very droll — the salt and pepper comes out of the eyes and mouth. $15.00-18.00.

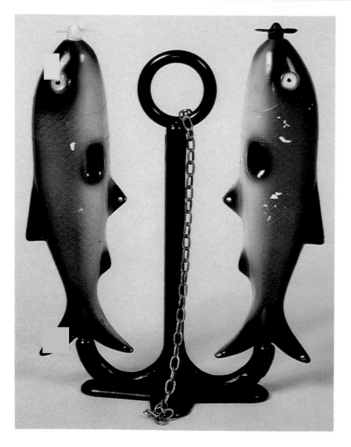

Things

Top: Anthropomorphic playing cards. MSR Imports — 1988. $15.00-18.00.

Center: Garbage cans personalized (why?) Shoe houses. $8.00-10.00 per pair.

Bottom: Pan and tea kettle in house stand. $30.00-40.00. Iron "people"; these are part of a series — typewriter head people, etc. They are pictured in the chapter on Series in my third book, p. 127. These have the same eyes. PY Japan. $45.00-55.00.

Top: The spoon and fork people are fairly common in the salt and pepper shakers, but harder to find in the vinegar and oil cruet combination. The heads have corks attached and are the stoppers for the cruets. Complete set. $30.00-40.00.

Center: Clock and broom and dust pan people — part of the series of household helpers. PY Japan. $45.00-55.00. Anthropomorphic pans hanging from a rolling pin stand, complete with measuring spoons and pastry brush. $24.00-28.00.

Bottom: Teapot people — heads and full body. $18.00-24.00 per pair.

Top: The strawberry heads are from Germany; wonderful expressions. $20.00-24.00. Flower heads (another series?) $10.00-12.00.

Upper Center: Other objects with faces — I love the cowboy hats! $20.00-30.00.

Lower Center: These telephones have eyes, a mouth, and an arm; they are chalk. $10.00-15.00.

Bottom: Another teapot head — different color and eyes. $18.00-24.00. Peanut people. $12.00-15.00 per pair.

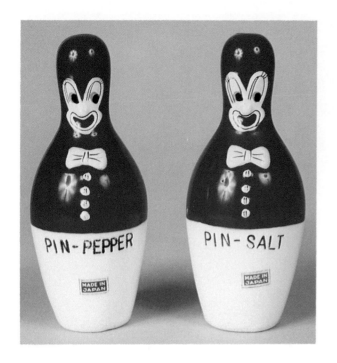

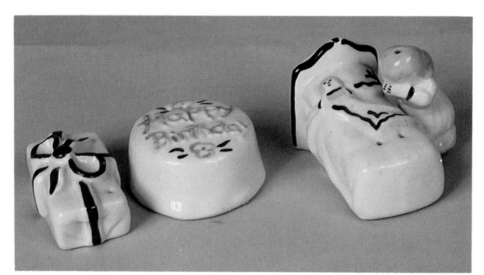

Top Left: Bowling pin people. $12.00-15.00.

Top Right: This is a maxi — larger than a mini but smaller than full size — album on table. $18.00-22.00.

Center: Birthday cake is also maxi — larger than a mini. $14.00-18.00. Girl saying her prayers with her doll in bed. $14.00-18.00.

Bottom: I found the same package with a birthday cake, and with a Sear's catalog. There is a Sear's catalog with an outhouse, but this might be another combination. $10.00-12.00. Baseballs on stands. $12.00-14.00.

Top: Hats and guns — nice quality glazes. $12.00-15.00 per pair.

Upper Center: Baseball set — the cap is attached to the bat, and the ball to the mitt. $18.00-22.00. Moon and rocket. $15.00-18.00.

Lower Center: These are unusual — they look like books on a stand or like paintings on an easel. $15.00-18.00.

Bottom: Telephone — real 1950's colors. $14.00-18.00. Bookends. $8.00-10.00.

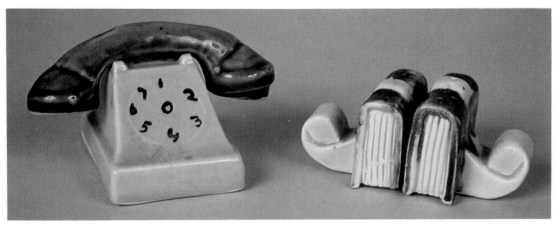

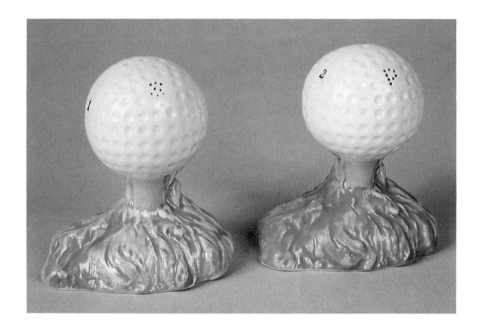

Top Left: Lighthouses. $8.00-12.00.

Top Right: Heavy ceramic graters — very realistic. $15.00-18.00.

Center: Golf balls on tees; golf items, like baseball, appeal to two different categories of collector. $15.00-18.00.

Bottom: These two sets are also maxis: nose and eye and pie and rolling pin. $10.00-12.00 per pair.

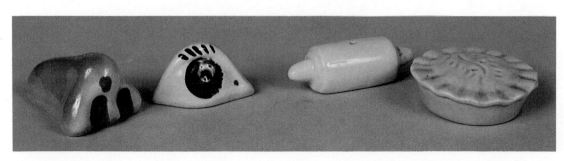

Top: Magnet and bar; gun and holster. These are also called "go-withs." $15.00-18.00.

Upper Center: Houses. $8.00-10.00. Dog goes all the way through his doghouse — very comic. $14.00-18.00.

Lower Center: Cigarettes and matches. $12.00-18.00. Telephone and directory. $10.00-12.00.

Bottom: These are not figural, but are examples of nice range sets from the 1930's-1950's. $15.00-18.00. The grease jar was often part of a set with lard container. $30.00-35.00.

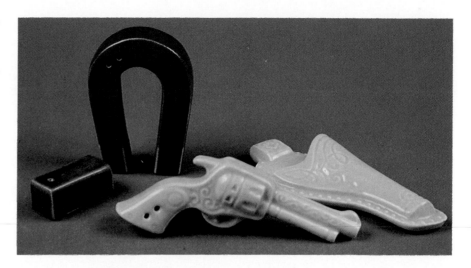

Top: Playing cards. $10.00-15.00. Deco dog with cigarettes as shakers. $25.00-35.00.

Upper Center: This ink blot and ink is by Treasure Craft; it is so great I would call it a classic. $35.00-45.00.

Lower Center: These black and white Deco heads are beautiful (Sarsaparilla) $25.00-35.00. The masks of comedy and tragedy. $15.00-20.00.

Bottom: Truck with logs and wagon with star. $16.00-20.00.

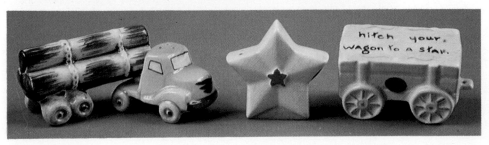

Top: Pig on scale. $18.00-22.00. Thumb on scale. $22.00-28.00.

Center: Sneakers, marked "Hot Shot" — special for Michael's photography studio. $10.00-12.00. Bowling trophies, marked Milwaukee, Wisc. $15.00-18.00.

Bottom: Trains in three sizes: mini, maxi, and standard. $14.00-28.00. Mini. $25.00-35.00

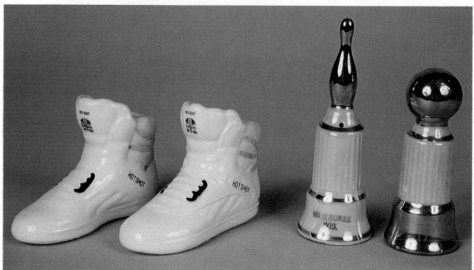

Top: More egg cups — the pair with the baseball cap is by Napco. $35.00-40.00.

Center: These are combination egg cups and salt and pepper shakers. $35.00-40.00.

Bottom: Spatter looking coffee pot on stove — both ceramic. $12.00-18.00. Desk and chair. The Good Company. $10.00-12.00.

Top: In this section the sets are almost the same, but made of different material. The larger set of milk cans is wood; the other metal. $10.00-12.00.

Upper Center: The identical set — even to the saying on top: "We're a Perfect Match." The pair with the print in red is the ceramic, the other is plastic, and came in the box. $12.00-15.00 per pair.

Lower Center: Three sets of coffee grinders; the largest is composition, the next is wood and the smallest is metal. $12.00-18.00 per pair.

Bottom: The captain and the whale are also the same, but one set is metal, the other wood. $15.00-18.00.

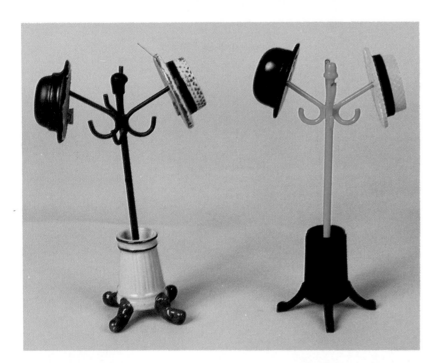

Top: The cowboy with the black hat is metal — the one with white hat is pottery. . . in both sets the hat is one shaker, the head the other. $20.00-25.00 per pair.

Center: The hat rack is probably the most common of the 1950's plastic sets; but I had never before seen the set in ceramic. Plastic, $10.00-12.00. Ceramic set, $25.00-35.00.

Bottom: Music notes in ceramic, and plastic notes on a metal stand. $15.00-18.00 per pair.

Tomorrow's Collectibles

Football. Clay Art of San Francisco, California, has been in existence for 13 years. They produce for both the Collector Market and the Mass Market. They strive to be both innovative and unique in their designs and humor is an integral part of their line. Their sets are designed by Ginny McLain and Tom Biela. Prices quoted are the new retail price; many go up in price drastically as soon as they are discontinued.

Top: Jack-in-the-box and Humpty Dumpty — beautiful glazes and colors. $16.00-18.00.

Upper Center: Golfer and bowler. $16.00-18.00.

Bottom: Flamingo Love and Earth on chair. $15.00-18.00.

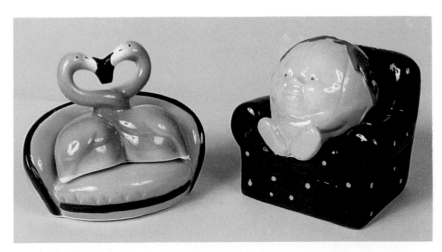

Top: Sunbathing tourist. $16.00-18.00

Upper Center: Red Riding Hood with the wolf in bed; fruit band. $15.00-18.00.

Lower Center: Catfish and cow bride and groom. $15.00-18.00.

Bottom: Two Christmas sets. $17.00-19.00.

Top: Coffee Break and rooster and sun. $16.00-18.00.

Upper Center: Bride and groom in car — the back says "just married." $16.00-18.00. Fortune teller. $16.00-18.00.

Lower Center: Clay Art has just come out with some stove top sets — much larger than the table size. They are 5½" x 4½". $25.00-30.00. Cow Gothic.

Bottom: The elephant is saying "eek, a mouse!" and the hippo is on the scale. $15.00-18.00.

Top: Chef and cool pig. $25.00-30.00.

Center: Penguins' night out and mother hen. $16.00-18.00.

Bottom: Cat at the piano. $15.00-18.00. Cat burglar and police dog. $16.00-18.00.

Sarsaparilla was an antique shop in New York City from 1968-78. They had lots of old salt and pepper shakers. In the early 1970's Andy Warhol bought lots of cookie jars and "kitsch" collectibles took off. In 1976 Sarsaparilla was incorporated as Sarsaparilla Deco Design with Les Sackin at its head, and they began manufacturing new "collectibles."

Top Left: Plane on earth and rocket ship. $15.00-18.00.

Top Right: Babies — one with lollipop and one crying. $14.00-18.00.

Center: Palette with paint brush. $14.00-16.00. Two part whale. $14.00-16.00.

Bottom: The Hollywood Mountain is a great landmark, and a great salt and pepper shaker — it splits in two horizontally. $13.00-15.00. Roll of $100 bills. $13.00-15.00.

Top: Typewriter on desk. $14.00-16.00. This sink and tub is by Omnibus. $12.00-14.00.

Center: Suntan lotion and Hollywood sun glasses. $14.00-16.00.

Bottom: Milk shake maker and milk shake. This is very realistic. $14.00-16.00.

Top: Bride and groom on china bench designed by Margo Sackin for Sarsaparilla. $14.00-18.00.

Center: Cowboy boots and saddle with original box by Sarsparilla. $15.00.

Vandor is another company currently manufacturing a lot of great salt and pepper shakers. The company is 35 years old, was originally based in San Francisco, and about four years ago it moved to Salt Lake City, Utah. They started making salt and pepper shakers about 10 years ago, and they are now an integral part of their line.

Bottom: Keeping up with the craze for cowboys and things western, Vandor not only designed some great cowboy and Indian sets, but also some great boxes. The cowboy's hat is one shaker, his head the other — real cord. Indian and tepee. $16.00-18.00 per pair.

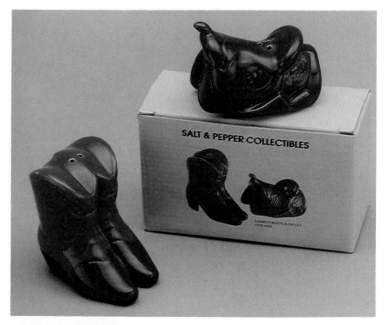

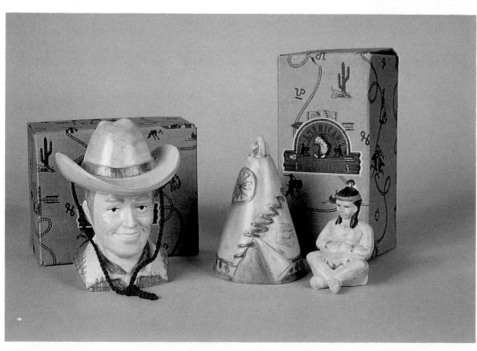

Top: Champagne and bucket. $15.00-18.00. Top hat. $15.00-18.00.

Victorian Memories is another line by Vandor with great boxes.

Center: Mother Cat with kittens in cradle, and cat in Victorian shoe. $16.00-18.00.

Bottom: Baseball Collectibles are hotter than ever; in fact I just saw this set in Cooperstown, New York where the Baseball Hall of Fame is. $16.00-18.00.

Top: This is one of my all time favorites: the parasol is one shaker and fits in the crocodile's hand. $15.00-18.00. The set in the center is by Clay Art and is called Gator Tourists. $16.00-18.00. The set on the far right is very funny — showing an alligator bell hop with an alligator suitcase. (Bet the former alligator didn't think it was so funny.) $15.00-18.00.

Center: Teddy bears on couch by Vandor. $16.00-18.00.

Bottom: Mona Lisa — another new set by Vandor. $16.00-18.00.

Top Pair of upright hands. $10.00-14.00. Hand on piano keyboard by Vandor. $15.00-18.00.

Center: Binoculars with leopard print — part of Vandor's Jungle theme. $16.00-18.00. Football players by Clay Art. $15.00-18.00.

Bottom: One base — two heads. $15.00-18.00. These all white pigs are Fitz and Floyd. $18.00-22.00.

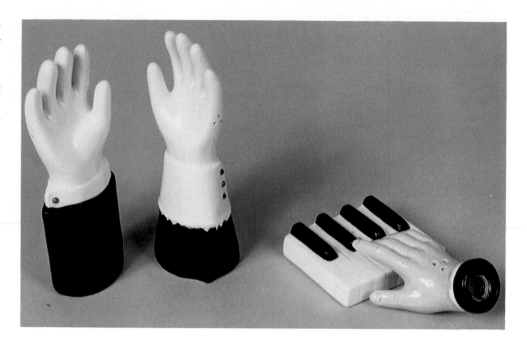

Top: Musical pigs by Otagiri; also the chef pigs. $14.00-16.00 per pair.

Center: Dressed mice by Otagiri. $15.00-18.00. Mouse and pumpkin. $14.00-18.00.

Bottom: Ham and Eggs — chicken and pig by Fitz and Floyd. $18.00-22.00. Serving cats also by Fitz and Floyd. $18.00-22.00.

Top Left: Pigs dining out by Clay Art. $15.00-18.00.

Top Right: Chicken McNugget by Dept. 56. $18.00-22.00.

Upper Center: Car with boat trailer. $15.00-18.00. Penguin couple in wooden boat. $20.00-22.00.

Lower Center: Dressed up pigs and rabbits by Otagiri. $15.00-18.00.

Bottom: Dinosaurs — called Steve and Edie by Fitz and Floyd. $18.00-22.00. Frogs by Otagiri. $14.00-16.00.

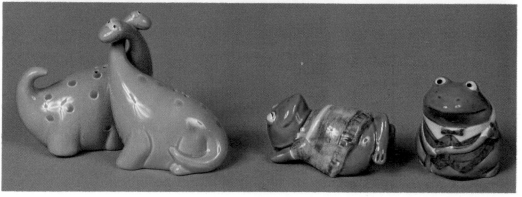

Top Left and Right: The jazz singer and Temptation by Clay Art. $15.00-18.00.

Center: Barbecue and Dalmatian. $16.00-18.00. Bark-o-lounger. $16.00-18.00.

Bottom: Cauliflower — looks good enough to eat — Fitz and Floyd. $16.00-18.00.

Top: Black and white chef by Sarsaparilla. $14.00-16.00. "Someone's Kitchen" by Design 50. (these have no faces). $18.00-22.00.

Center: Cows. $8.00-10.00. Cow jumping over the moon. Clay Art. $15.00-18.00.

Bottom: Cat's pyjamas and mother cat and kittens both by Clay Art. $15.00-18.00.

Top: Cinderella's slipper on pillow by Applause. $20.00-24.00. Charlie Brown and Lucy on chair, Charles Schulz by Willitts Design. $75.00-85.00.

Center: Roller skate and popcorn, and hamburger and french fries by Freelance, Inc. Dayton New Jersey. $10.00-12.00 per pair.

Bottom: Ice cream sodas and car hops also by Freelance, Inc. $10.00-12.00.

Top: Grocery carts that really roll with salt and pepper. Peanut butter and jelly, and one other I saw but didn't get; milk and Oreo cookies. (by Applause). $15.00 per pair.

Center: Milk bottles in holder by Ron Gordon Designs. $12.00-14.00.

Bottom: Tropical juice container and car and gas pump by Ron Gordon Designs, Paterson, New Jersey. $12.00-14.00.

Top: Maid and butler — Kessler (called "Full Staff"). $10.00-12.00.

Center: Rabbit with bunch of carrots and a pair of rabbits also a Kessler. $10.00-12.00.

Bottom: Cat in cup by Clay Art — cats are always popular! $15.00-18.00. Pair of cats by Albert Kessler, San Franisco, California. $10.00-12.00.

All of the following fruits and vegetables by Albert Kessler make a lovely permanent centerpiece arranged in a wicker basket.

Top: Watermelons and apples. $10.00-12.00.

Center: Green peppers and eggplants. $10.00-12.00.

Bottom: Asparagus and white onions. $10.00-12.00.

Top: Corn, bananas, and radishes. $10.00-12.00.

Bottom: A pair of cottages amd a rabbit with wheelbarrow — Kessler. $10.00-12.00.

Top: Crocodile in a rubber raft. $15.00-18.00. Black couple dancing. $24.00-28.00.

Center: New for Sarsaparilla. Eagle and binoculars. Giraffes. $12.00-14.00.

Bottom: Mailboxes and ketchup and mustard by Ron Gordon. $12.00-14.00.

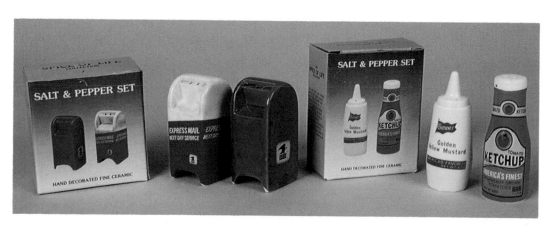

About the Author...

Helene Guarnaccia has been interested in antiques all of her adult life, and lives with early pine furniture and blue and white willowware — her first dinner set was Fiesta.

Helene taught high school Spanish for 20 years, and took early retirement in order to pursue her interest in collecting. This is her fourth book on salt and pepper shakers, and she is currently at work on a price guide for Collector Books on snow domes.

Helene collects plastic windup toys, nesting figures, and measuring spoon holders.

She has two sons and three grandchildren and lives with her husband, Paul, in Fairfield, Connecticut.